FOOTBALL
Startling Stories
Behind the Records

FOOTBALL
Startling Stories
Behind the Records

Jim Benagh
of *The New York Times*
Sports department
and Sports Editor of the
"Guinness Book of World Records"

 Sterling Publishing Co., Inc.   **New York**

$12.49

Library of Congress Cataloging-in-Publication Data

Benagh, Jim, 1937-
   Football, startling stories behind the records / Jim Benagh.
      p.   cm.
   Includes index.
   Summary: Recounts true incidents which occurred before and during
college and professional football games in the United States, in
such categories as "Team Efforts" and "Extra Points."
   ISBN 0-8069-6618-1.   ISBN 0-8069-6619-X (lib. bdg.)
   1. Football—United States—Juvenile literature.   [1. Football—
History.   2. Football—Records.]   I. Title.
GV950.7.B43   1987
796.332'0973—dc 19   87-17334
                                                          CIP
                                                          AC

1   3   5   7   9   10   8   6   4   2

Copyright © 1987 by Jim Benagh
Published by Sterling Publishing Co., Inc.
Two Park Avenue, New York, N.Y. 10016
Distributed in Canada by Oak Tree Press Ltd.
% Canadian Manda Group, P.O. Box 920, Station U
Toronto, Ontario, Canada M8Z 5P9
Distributed in the United Kingdom by Blandford Press
Link House, West Street, Poole, Dorset BH15 1LL, England
Distributed in Australia by Capricorn Ltd.
P.O. Box 665, Lane Cove, NSW 2066
Manufactured in the United States of America
All rights reserved
Sterling ISBN 0-8069-6618-1 Trade
                    6619-X Library

Contents

Introduction   *7*

I. **Making Their Points**   *9*
Point-A-Minute Teams *9* • 11 TD's In One
College Game *14* • A Touchdown Splurge
Like None Other in College History *17* •
Held Scoring Records for 3 Pro Teams *23* •
One Player, 899 Points *24* • 37 Touchdowns
in His Freshman Year *28* • Long-Distance
Touchdown Record *29*

II. **By Air and Land**   *32*
Student Manager Scored a Point *32* •
7 Unexpected Touchdown Passes in One
NFL Game *34* • A Super Performance *37*
• 18 Passes Caught in One NFL Game *41*
• When Opportunity Knocked, He Caught
Passes for 309 Yards *44* • 10 TD Passes in
a College Game *48* • Almost 10 Yards
Every Carry *50* • Quarterback Rushed 38
Times in One Game *53* • First to Top 2,000
Yards Rushing *56*

III. **Just for Kicks**   *59*
NFL Field-Goal Record on His First
Try *59* • Averaged 52.7-Yard Punts Same
Day as 46-Yard Field Goal *61* • Long Field
Goal Without His Shoe On *63* • 17 Field
Goals in a College Freshman Game *64* •
Punted 98 Yards in an NFL Game *66* •
Percentage Kicker *70*

IV. Witnesses for the Defense *73*

Blocked a Field Goal at the Crossbar *73* •
Blocked 3 Punts in a Single Pro Game *76* •
Scored 2 TDs on Blocked Punts *77* •
4 Interception Returns for TDs *78* •
Averaged Over One Interception a Game
in College Career *79* • Nailed 2 Pro QBs
for Safeties Within 5 Minutes *80* • Did Not
Play College Football But Played 170
Straight Games as a Pro *81* • Recovered 4
Straight Onside Kicks *83*

V. Team Efforts *84*

73-0 Bears *84* • 222-0 Comedy *87* • Won
78 Consecutive Games *90* • Undefeated,
Untied and Unscored-On *91* • 53 Pro Football
Candidates in College One Season *94* •
Alabama Is Bowl Bound *95* • Prolific Scoring
Prep Teams *98*

VI. Extra Points *99*

Figured in Every NFL Statistical
Category *99* • Speed "King of the
Hill" *103* • The Mrs. Played Pro Football
108 • A Full 60 Minutes in 3 Consecutive
Rose Bowls *110* • Seven Brothers Played
for Same Old-Time Pro Team *112* • A
National Championship in First Year as
Head Coach *114* • Coached Unbeaten
High-School Team when Just 19 Years
Old *117* • The National Football League's
One-Game Wonders *119*

**Roster of Players and
Teams** *121*

Introduction

Football is not the statistical sport in the sense that baseball is, which is one more reason why I enjoy researching football. Facts don't come as easily and the challenge is greater.

For that same reason, there are more things to uncover in gridiron lore. I remember when a player from my high school, Tommy McGinn in Cheboygan, Michigan, scored 153 points in his senior year and 350 for his career. I was impressed enough to try to find out whether it was a state record, and it was. Yet a few years later, I found out that same year, 1953, Ken Hall of Sugar Land, Texas, got 395, to say nothing of 899 in his career.

But more than just numbers are the stories behind them, some even startling. Like the player who set a field-goal record on his first attempt, a star like Red Grange who scored four long touchdown runs in the first 12 minutes of his biggest college game, or a player who scored 71 points in a college game, even though the school has no record of his enrollment. Even a woman who played professional football. One story I dug out of a dusty upstairs of a library in Wheeling, West Virginia, when several letters and phone calls proved fruitless.

This book is a collection of many of those stories behind the records, and in some cases stories behind some unofficial records, or what some critics might call non-records, such as a student manager coming off the bench to score. But they're all records in my book.

Jim Benagh

• I •
Making Their Points

Point-A-Minute Teams

Perhaps no football team in history dominated an era as the University of Michigan's "Point-A-Minute" teams did from 1901 through 1905. For that period, the Wolverines scored a total of 2,821 points in 57 games—an average of 49.5 per outing. If they fell short of making a full 60 points per game, they could be excused. Many games were called before the regulation end in order to spare downtrodden opponents further embarrassment. Furthermore, the touchdowns which Michigan scored in bunches were worth only five points in those days.

Michigan had fielded a normal football team in 1900, one that posted a 7-2-1 record and scored 117 points. Then Michigan hired Fielding H. (Hurry Up) Yost to coach the Wolverines, and the course of football history was changed. In his 1901 debut on the Ann Arbor campus, Yost's team ran up 50 points on a surprised Albion College team. Four weeks later, they tallied 128 against Buffalo. In another game, they had 89.

Their amazing scoring machine was invited to visit Pasadena and play Stanford University in what would be the forerunner of post-season bowl games on New Year's Day, 1902. Michigan agreed to make the trip to the Tournament of Roses, but after training in snowy Ann Arbor the team found the hot West Coast weather much to its disadvantage.

Against Stanford, the Wolverines got off to a sluggish start. Both teams traded punts and field position back and forth for about 23 minutes. Then Willie Heston, a halfback and the greatest star of the Point-A-Minute era, broke loose with a run that set up a touchdown. Michigan grabbed a half-time lead of 17-0.

The second half was a walk-through as Michigan could not be stopped. Heston didn't score a TD, but he gained nearly 200 of Michigan's 504 yards. Teammate Neil Snow scored five times. When the score reached 49-0 with several minutes to play, Michigan had yet to substitute, and Stanford players were getting injured one after the other. The game was called by mutual agreement.

For the season, Michigan had swept past 11 opponents, scoring 550 points. It would be the Wolverines' *lowest* total until 1905, when they scored 495. No one scored on Michigan in 1901.

In 1902, Michigan outscored the opposition, 644-12 in 11 games. In 1903, it was 565-6, though a tie with Minnesota spoiled an otherwise unblemished record. In 1904, the Wolverines were unbeaten again, outscoring opponents 567-22 in 10 games.

That was Heston's last year. In four seasons, he had scored 72 five-point touchdowns, far more than anyone in college football history. He had never played in a losing game.

But the Wolverines, who had topped 100 points four

The greatest star on one of college football's greatest teams, Willie Heston, scored more touchdowns in his college days than most teams do.

times with Willie in the lineup, learned to live without him in 1905. For most of the season, they did nicely. In

The Point-A-Minute Teams

1901

Mich.		Opp.
50	Albion	0
57	Case Tech	0
33	Indiana	0
29	Northwestern....	0
128	Buffalo..........	0
22	Carlisle	0
21	Ohio State	0
22	Chicago	0
89	Beloit...........	0
50	Iowa............	0
49	Stanford*	0

*Rose Bowl

1902

Mich.		Opp.
88	Albion	0
48	Case Tech	6
119	Michigan State ..	0
60	Indiana	0
23	Notre Dame	0
86	Ohio State	0
6	Wisconsin	0
107	Iowa............	0
21	Chicago	0
63	Oberlin	0
23	Minnesota	6

1903

Mich.		Opp.
31	Case Tech	0
79	Beloit...........	0
65	Ohio Northern ...	0
51	Indiana	0
88	Ferris Inst.......	0
47	Drake...........	0
76	Albion	0
6	Minnesota	6
36	Ohio State	0
16	Wisconsin	0
42	Oberlin	0
28	Chicago	0

1904

Mich.		Opp.
33	Case Tech	0
48	Ohio Northern ...	0
95	Kalamazoo.......	0
72	Chicago P. & S. ..	0
31	Ohio State	6
72	Amer. Medical ...	0
130	West Va.	0
28	Wisconsin	0
36	Drake...........	4
22	Chicago	12

1905

Mich.		Opp.
65	Ohio Wesleyan ...	0
44	Kalamazoo.......	0
36	Case Tech	0
23	Ohio Northern ...	0
18	Vanderbilt.......	0
31	Nebraska	0
70	Albion	0
48	Drake...........	0
33	Illinois	0
40	Ohio State	0
12	Wisconsin	0
75	Oberlin	0
0	Chicago	2

their first 12 games, the Wolverines were unbeaten and unscored-on, and scored 495 points. Then in the season finale, Michigan lost to Chicago, 2-0. It was the first defeat in 57 games.

In five years, Michigan gave up only six TDs, and only two of them came as the result of sustained drives.

During that time, Michigan topped 100 points per game four times, including a high of 130 versus West Virginia; it topped 80 points five other times. All in all, Michigan went over the coveted 60-point mark 20 times, including a 75-point splurge the week before it lost to Chicago.

Never again would college football see such scoring. But in their next trip to the Rose Bowl, in 1948, Michigan offered a reminder of days gone by. The Wolverines won, 49-0, again.

11 TD's in One College Game

The Sunday sports pages of November 20, 1932, were about as bleak as the fog and snow that blanketed the playing fields of the nation's colleges the day before. Yale beat Harvard in "The Game" by a whopping but dull 19-0 score, the largest margin in three decades between the teams. Old Man Stagg closed out his 41-year career at the University of Chicago with a disappointing loss to Wisconsin. Even the pros were uninteresting. The old New York *Herald-Tribune* had predicted that the feature N.F.L. battle between the New York Giants and the Green Bay Packers would be "the most attractive game on the home list," but saw fit to give the contest only three paragraphs on page eight.

If there was any bright football news that dull day, it had to be a report out of Wheeling, West Virginia, where a small-college freshman made football history. His name was Joe Korshalla. The papers heralded his feats in their front sports pages—and spelled his name "Kershalla."

Joe Korshalla was a bowling ball type of halfback of Polish-Slavic descent from the coal mining country near Wilkes-Barre, Pennsylvania, who wound up on the campus of West Liberty Normal a few years after he got out of high school. "Cueball" Korshalla had been a big name in high school, but his contributions to West Liberty football in 1932 were minimal—until November 19. He had scored only one touchdown from his post at halfback. The fuzzy newspaper reports of that season say he was often injured.

But West Liberty's final opponent of the year, Cedarville College, was ripe for a bright performance by Korshalla and the other West Liberty Hilltoppers. Cedarville's Yellowjackets had been outscored, 268-7, in their previous seven losses. Korshalla was the first Hilltop-per to take advantage of Cedarville's discouraged legions. The first time he got the ball, in the opening minute of play, he rambled 70 yards for a touchdown. It set the tone for West Liberty that day. Every time the Hilltoppers got the ball in the first half, they scored. As the half neared completion, and Cedarville neared depletion, it was mutually decided to cut the playing time of the game. The first half would be only 24 minutes instead of the normal 30; the second half would consist of two ten-minute quarters.

Even then, West Liberty had an 83-0 halftime lead and Korshalla had racked up six TDs, none of them shorter than 22 yards.

In the second half, West Liberty got more benevolent and pulled out its first stringers except for Korshalla. That didn't stop Cueball from rolling to one-game collegiate records for TDs, points and yards rushing. He made four more TDs going into the final minute of the shortened 44-minute game. Also along the way, he kicked five extra points. Then in the waning seconds, he got off a 75-yard punt return for his eleventh TD. But it was called back because of a clipping penalty by a teammate who was playing his first game. West Liberty held Cedarville, though, and got the ball back. Korshalla ran from scrimmage one last time and went 35 for a TD that counted.

The game ended but the statisticians didn't.

It took more than three hours to sort through the maze of figures and find out just exactly what West Liberty and Korshalla had done—besides winning 137-0.

The official tallies credited Korshalla with 11 TDs, none of them less than 22 yards and most of them over 40; five extra points; and 504 yards rushing in 20 carries.

The 71 points were 3 better than the collegiate

record, set by another West Liberty player the year before.

Then Korshalla disappeared from the college football scene almost as fast as he arrived. The school—now West Liberty State—admits that he may not have been a student after all; the official historian can find no proof that he was ever enrolled. "It might be that he was a ringer," Art Barbeau, who claimed to be the "official drum beater" for West Liberty sports, said a few years ago. When asked if Korshalla had any teammates who could solve the mystery, Barbeau replied: "Try a guy over in Follansbee. He played for West Liberty eight straight years."

Korshalla's widow was tracked down in Pennsylvania, and even she was at a loss to explain why her husband, who had died several years ago, used two different spellings for his last name. "He didn't talk much about football," she said.

The next fall, 1933, a new football coach was in and scholarships were out—a Depression kid could no longer trade his sports talent for room and board at West Liberty. But Joe Korshalla left another mark before he packed his bags and returned to the coal country. In the spring of 1933, West Liberty Normal met Rio Grande College in a baseball doubleheader. The next day, the Sunday papers were reporting how a Joe Kershalla, batting clean-up, smacked four triples for what may be another record of some sort.

A Touchdown Splurge
Like None Other in College History

He was an improbable hero from the most remarkable period in sports history—the 1920s. It was a time when Babe Ruth was swatting tape-measure home runs, when Jack Dempsey was scoring tremendous knockouts, when Bobby Jones was attacking pars in golf, when Paavo Nurmi was assaulting records in track, when Bill Tilden was dominating tennis. It was called "The Golden Age of Sports," a time when sports came of age.

But the most exciting figure at the time in this crazed era of fandom was an introverted college kid who did not go looking for the pile of publicity that would bury him in hero worship.

His name was Harold Grange, but better known as Red because of his burnt-blond hair. Never in history has there been so much adulation heaped on a single athlete as there was on Red Grange in the 1920s, even though he was the youngest of this Golden Age of heroes.

Grange was a smalltown boy from Wheaton, Illinois, who had ventured downstate to get an education at the University of Illinois. He was quiet, almost shy, and he certainly wasn't looking to be a campus hero, much less a national one. In fact, though he was a pretty good high

"Red" Grange turns the corner against Michigan on one of his record-making touchdowns.

school football player, he was more interested in basketball and track—two less glamorous sports—when he enrolled at Illinois.

It was only because fraternity brothers knew of his high school reputation that they insisted—not asked, but ordered—that he play football. From the time he went out for the team, there was magic.

It didn't hurt that he was given the number 77 when he made the varsity. Even that was by accident. As Grange liked to recall, "I got it because the guy before me got No. 76 and the guy behind me in line got No. 78."

Playing for the first time in 1923 as a sophomore, Grange literally took off. He scored three touchdowns, including a 66-yard run, and gained 208 yards in his first game, against a good Nebraska team. The Illini, with Grange running for 175 yards, stopped Iowa's long winning streak and behind Grange's 160 yards gave Chicago its only loss. Against Northwestern, he gained 251 yards in just 19 minutes of playing time, and for the season he ran 1,260 yards in just seven games. He made everybody's All-America team, and was the football hero fans were looking for to fit nicely into the 1920's mold of star. Remember at that time, pro football held little or no interest thoughout the country. College ball was the game and Grange was the man.

Through a quirk in the schedule, Illinois and Michigan, fellow members of the Big Ten Conference, did not meet in 1923 and both went undefeated, sharing the conference title. That set up an even bigger game—and more publicity for Grange—in 1924 when they were scheduled to play in Illinois' Memorial Stadium.

But the pressure that went on on the field was nothing compared with what was happening to Grange's life out of uniform. Here was a youngster getting a thousand letters a month from adoring fans. Many came from female admirers he never met—or wanted to meet. Newsreel men barged into his fraternity house to live with him for two or three days at a time. Even in summertime, vacation time for some, all he wanted to do was go back to his little farm town of Wheaton and work on the ice wagon that helped him to strengthen his God-given legs. But reporters and photographers were there, too, asking him to raise 100-pound chunks of ice for the camera as they dubbed him "the Wheaton Iceman." He was better known by the nickname "The Galloping Ghost," because of his zigzagging movements on the field.

There were other pressures more football-related. As a student editor of the *Michigan Daily*, a school paper, wrote when he left Grange off his all-star team, "All Grange can do is run." To which an Illinois writer retorted in his school paper, "All Galli-Curci can do is sing." Galli-Curci just happened to be the leading lady opera star of the time.

The Illini were further disturbed during the summer of 1924 when the famous Michigan coach, Fielding Yost, who was stepping out of coaching that year for health reasons, told a reporter, "Meester Grange will be a carefully watched man every time he takes the ball. There will be just about eleven clean, hard Michigan tacklers headed for him at the same time.

"I know he is a great runner, but great runners usually have the hardest time gaining ground when met by special preparation."

Needless to say, Bob Zuppke, the Illinois coach, had his scissors out and clipped everything for the team's bulletin board.

Yost scouted Grange's first game of the 1924 season, again against Nebraska. For the first time, Red was held scoreless, and though he gained a respectable 116 yards, it was below his standard. Illinois won but not easily, 7-6. Grange passed for the first time in that game, too, but Yost looked upon it as a possible decoy. Yost noted with joy that Grange could be knocked out of bounds when he broke into an "S" pattern to get his runs underway.

Illinois held Grange back in his next game, the warmup for the October 18 Michigan game. He played only 16 minutes as the Illini breezed to victory. Michigan, meanwhile, was winning two straight shutouts and looked as if it had another powerful defense, maybe something better than Grange had faced as a sophomore.

The stage was set, and so was the audience, for the showdown. A crowd of 66,609, the largest ever to see a game in the Midwest, was on hand on game day, as were the nation's most prominent sportswriters.

Michigan made the decision at the start of the game to let Grange have the ball. The Wolverines chose to kick off, rather than receive, and put their fate in the hands of their defense. Zuppke had a strategy of his own, too. Instead of having his kickoff returner, Grange, race up the sideline, he had him go up the middle of the field.

Grange got the kickoff and headed for the right sideline, as the Wolverines expected. But there would be no knocking him out of bounds. In fact, no one touched him as he cut back to the center of the field. He went 95 yards for the touchdown the first time he handled the ball against a Michigan team.

Sticking to their game plan, the Wolverines chose to kick off again, rather than receive. This time they stopped Grange on the 20 and after an Illini penalty and punt, the strategy seemed to be working. But the Wolverines had to give up the ball on downs.

Illinois gave the ball to another runner on its first

play from scrimmage, and it was good for only 3 yards. Then it was Grange's turn again.

This time, he took off around left end, broke into the clear and picked up his blockers. He cut back sharply, using the wall of blockers, threw a hip fake on the safety man and was gone, 67 yards and a touchdown.

Michigan remain unconvinced.

Again the Wolverines decided to kick off. The teams stopped each other from scrimmage and were forced to punt.

When No. 77 got the ball, he was off and running again, this time for a 56-yard touchdown run around end.

Undaunted but down by 20-0, Michigan decided once more to keep Illinois deep in its territory and kicked off. This time it went into the end zone. Grange was smothered on the next play and soon the Illini punted. The Wolverine strategy was taking hold. But perhaps the Wolverines were not as confident as their coach. They fumbled the punt, lost it and soon Grange was headed for the end zone, this time an end run for 44 yards. The game was a mere 12 minutes old.

Grange was given a well-earned rest after that one.

Zuppke saw him panting as he leaned on the goal post and figured that in 12 minutes he had gained about 300 yards, added maybe 100 more going sideways and uncountable more yards going back and forth to get into position after touchdowns. He knew Grange was a speedster not a distanceman, so he sat him down till the second half.

But Grange was not done for the day. In the second half, he had another touchdown, this one for 15 yards, and threw a touchdown pass.

When his day's work was tallied up, he had 402 yards in 21 carries and passed for 64 more yards.

Illinois won the grudge game, 39-14.

Held Scoring Records
for 3 Pro Teams

As ageless George Blanda approached his 25th professional football season in 1974, he spoke about the art
of place-kicking. "It's conceivable that I could kick
forever," he said. "Physically, playing golf is tougher."

It seems that George Blanda, who would retire after
the 1975 season, had indeed been playing forever. The
second game of the 1973 season was his 300th as a professional. His 26 seasons are far and away more than
any other player recorded. One of the runnersup, Johnny
Unitas, in fact, has introduced George at banquets as
"my boyhood hero." Blanda played in 340 games.

Place-kicking, of course, is what has kept Blanda active for so long. He's been somewhat of a "relief pitcher"
as a quarterback while in his forties, a feat that helped
earn him Player of the Year honors as late as 1970. But
as far as moving the ball is concerned, he hadn't scored
a touchdown since 1960.

Kicking the ball was a Blanda specialty since he
came into pro football with the Chicago Bears in 1949.
His records are too numerous to list. But his greatest
feat may be that of once holding the all-time scoring
records for three teams.

Blanda left the Chicago Bears in 1958. But he took
the Bear record of 541 points with him.

Blanda sat out the 1959 season. People thought he
was over the hill at age 32. But he came back with the
new Houston Oiler team of the American Football
League in 1960. He came close to leading the AFL in
scoring that first campaign with 115 points. Before the
Oilers gave up on him in 1966, he established a team
record of 598 points that still stands.

The Oakland Raiders were quick to pick up Blanda as a back-up quarterback and place-kicker. He did not disappoint them in either category, becoming famous for his last-minute heroics as a clutch passer and kicker. At one stretch, he made 201 conversions in a row, third best streak in League history. He scored a team-record 703 points in seven seasons as a Raider.

Altogether, Blanda scored 2,002 points as a pro. Along with nine touchdowns, he made 943 of 959 points-after-touchdowns and 335 of 638 field goals. Nine of his field goals have traveled 50 yards or more.

All-time runnerup Jan Stenerud had 1,699 points. How great are Blanda's records?

A place-kicker in these days of the specialist is considered to have a fine season if he scores 100 points in a year, as Blanda did in 1973. A newcomer in the league would thus need about 20 fine seasons to catch up with him.

One Player, 899 Points

Kenneth Hall of Sugar Land (Texas) High School could do just about anything he wanted as a high school football star. Consider, for example, his greatest game for the small-town team on the outskirts of Houston. It was 1953, Hall's senior year, and he was setting records that no prep has come close to matching to this day. Hall was aiming for the State one-game scoring record of 48 points set by a Dick Todd, who had tallied 318 points in one season and 664 in his career at Crowell High.

Hall matched the 48 with time to play against Houston Lutheran. En route to that total, he had rushed for 520 yards in only 11 attempts, for an average of 47.3 a try, and returned a kickoff 64 yards and a punt 82 yards for TDs. As Sugar Land's place-kicker, Hall knew that

Todd's single game record was within reach. But as Sugar Land lined up for the extra point, Hall, unbeknown to his teammates, took off running with the ball instead of kicking it. A 205-pounder with 9.7 speed in the 100-yard dash, he crossed the goal line.

The 49 points, as impressive as they were, hardly compared with Hall's other records. As a senior he scored 395 points in 12 games, including two State playoff contests. In his career, 841 came in his final three years, for a total of 899.

Hall rushed for 4,045 yards—about 337 a game—as a senior. He accumulated 11,232 in his prep career.

Surprisingly, this was after Hall got a belated start at Sugar Land. He didn't go out for football right away in his freshman year. But after the team lost its first three games, the principal assembled the boys among the 130 Sugar Land students and asked for their support. Hall and several other freshmen and sophomores answered the call. Sugar Land lost only one game by the time Hall graduated—and that loss came in a game when he did not play.

As a football newcomer, Hall was mostly used as a passer. But later he was installed at tailback for Coach L. V. Hightower's teams, taking the snap from center in the Sugar Land box formation about 5 yards behind the line of scrimmage. There was no stopping him.

Hightower often recalled the game against Orchard High, in which Hall called for a "box right" play whereby he would carry the ball. Hall went 80 yards for the TD. But the officials called it back because of a penalty. Hall called for a "box left" on the next play and went 85 yards to score.

It was after that second play that officials called for a timeout. Hightower, wondering why the ensuing kickoff was held up, summoned the officials for an ex-

Ken Hall's schoolboy scoring records have been as durable as they have been unbelieveable.

planation. No problem, they said, they were just tired out!

After completing his high school career, Hall went to Texas A&M. His bubble burst in a conflict of philosophy with Coach Paul (Bear) Bryant. Hall did not get to play much as a sophomore and dropped out of school. He signed a contract to play professionally in Canada and became a starter for the Canadian Football League champion Edmonton Eskimos.

A few years later, he returned to Houston to play for the Oiler team of the new American Football League. As an A.F.L. rookie, he got back into the record book again—this time with a 104-yard kickoff return. It is still a team record.

Ken Hall's Record

As a freshman in 1950, Ken Hall scored 58 points in 7 games. In 1951, 224 points in 12 games. In 1952, 222 points in 11 games. And finally in 1953, his record season, 395 points in 12 games. Below is a table of that incredible 1953 season.

Sugar Land Scores			Hall's Scores		
S.L.		Opp.	TDs	P.A.T.	Total Pts.
40	Katy	14	4	4	28
53	Missouri City	18	6	5	41
45	Needville	7	3	3	21
73	Houston Lutheran	14	7	7	49
41	Van Vleck	7	5	5	35
41	Klein	18	5	5	35
67	Orchard	19	5	7	37
59	Danbury	12	7	5	47
47	Pearland	13	4	5	29
46	Barber's Hill	12	6	3	39
	Playoff Games				
33	Chester	13	3	3	21
13	Magnolia	6	2	1	13
					395

37 Touchdowns in His Freshman Year

Wilbert Montgomery wasn't exactly what you would call a highly sought-after prospect during his senior year of high school in 1972. The reason was fairly simple: he played defensive back most of the time while his younger brother Cleotha handled the rushing chores at their Greenville, Mississippi, high school.

Montgomery found the end zone in college, however, after Abilene Christian College in Texas gave him a scholarship. In fact, he found it a record 37 times in 1973. Not since 1926, when a player named Mayes McLain of Haskell Institute had scored 38 times, had a player found the goal line so often in one season. But in 1926 collegiate records were unofficial.

The Abilene road-runner scored 31 of his TDs in regular-season play and led the team into the NAIA post-season tournament. He needed only nine games to top the modern college record in regular season play (29, by Lydell Mitchell, Penn State). Then, in the playoffs, he scored four times in a semifinal victory over Langston (Oklahoma) University and two more times against Elon (North Carolina) College as his team easily won the NAIA title. His 224 total points was another modern record.

For his first year, he rushed for 1,181 yards and averaged 6.5 yards a carry.

And that was not the last heard of Montgomery, who went on to star for the Philadelphia Eagles.

Billy (White Shoes) Johnson (right) was one of college football's and later the NFL's best long-distance runners. In college he broke several records, including one set by Colorado's Whizzer White, (left), now a Supreme Court Justice.

Long-Distance Touchdown Record

Billy Johnson was a 9.5 sprinter on the track team for little Widener College of Chester, Pennsylvania, in the 1970s. But by college football measuring sticks, he was a long-distance star.

A native of Marcus Hook, Pennsylvania, Johnson chose the college near his home because he wanted a nearby school where his father could see him play. He had to sit out his first season—1971—because of an eligibility problem, but he worked his way into the starting lineup as a sophomore in 1972. He sparkled right from the start. Carrying the ball about 10 times a game, he gained over 100 yards rushing for three straight weeks. He also scored two touchdowns in each of the games.

Coach Bill Manlove of Widener began wondering about the phenomenal prospect he had in the fold and a decision was made to move the 5' 8½", 170-pounder from slotback to running back. "We just weren't feeding him the ball enough," said Manlove. "But then we began wondering if he would be tough enough in the new position because he had difficulty gaining 100 yards there in a game. The week later we stopped wondering—he gained 200 yards."

As a slotback, Johnson had scored three TDs—averaging 32.3 yards for his jaunts. As a running back, he began ripping off touchdown runs of unbelievable lengths.

In three years on the varsity, Johnson would run from scrimmage for 51 touchdowns. The average length of his scoring bursts on rushes was 35.9 yards. As a punt returner, he dashed for seven more touchdowns, averaging 81.2 yards for each breakaway. He also returned one kickoff for 85 yards.

Altogether Billy Johnson scored 62 touchdowns in his college career, and the average length of those twisting, sprinting tallies was 41.7 yards—far and away an NCAA record. He also had seven other TDs called back because of penalties. Their average length: 60.0 yards.

As a ball-handler, Johnson scored a touchdown each 7.7 times he rushed, caught a pass, or returned a kick. That broke the mark set by West Point's Doc Blanchard (one TD per 8.2 attempts), who starred during the World War II years when Army had a monopoly on the best college players. Johnson also wiped out the record of 246.3 "all-purpose yards" set by another Hall of Fame star, Colorado's Whizzer White, the future Supreme Court Justice. Billy gained 251.6 yards on rushes, receptions and returns each game in one season.

All in all, Johnson set nine NCAA records.

• II •

By Air and Land

Student Manager Scored a Point

College football's unsung heroes, contrary to popular belief, are not the anonymous guards who pave the way for touchdown runs but the student managers who do all the dirty work around the football field. Their only rewards are association with the football team and possibly a special manager's monogram.

In 1952, however, Yale University gave its student manager, 140-pound Charley Yeager, a special bonus.

— It began as a lark, to loosen up a taut team during one of the Elis' better recent seasons. The team would throw passes to 5′ 6″ Charley in practice. After a while, Yale devised a fake extra-point play for him. The quarterback (the ball holder on the placement try) would get the snap from center, stand up and toss the ball to the eager Yeager. Yale even got a uniform—No. 99, the smallest one available—ready for him in case the game situation would dictate the prank play.

But as the Bulldogs rolled through the 1952 season, there was little hope that Charley would get into a game. As the season finale loomed ahead, against arch-rival Harvard, there seemed no chance at all. Yale and Harvard people call their contest "The Game" and treat it with gridiron reverence.

Still, Yeager got his name in the game program.

However, when the team packed its gear for the trip to Harvard Yeager had to do his chores as usual as student manager, heading the Yale staff in getting ready for the game.

When Yale rolled up a 27-7 lead by halftime, though, Charley was told to get into uniform. This might be his day. After Yale scored a third-quarter touchdown, the manager got the word from the head coach, Jordan Olivar, to be ready to go in if the Bulldogs made yet another touchdown.

The Yale players, sensing the excitement that would enliven a game seemingly won, worked hard to get another score right away—and they did. Little Charley Yeager dashed inconspicuously onto the field for the extra point scrimmage. He lined up at right end.

As the ball was snapped, Charley got knocked over by a Harvard player. Yale's quarterback saw that, but his other receivers were having trouble, too, so he went right. Charley bounced to his feet and continued into the end zone.

The quarterback tossed and Charley clutched the ball to his gut. He made his point for student managers all over the country.

7 Unexpected Touchdown Passes in One NFL Game

More than one pro football quarterback shares the NFL record of seven touchdown passes in a single game. But if ever there was an unlikely candidate for the record, it had to be the Minnesota Vikings' Joe Kapp in 1969.

Four players had accomplished the feat before Injun Joe Kapp stepped onto the field against the Baltimore Colts on September 28, 1969. Their names were Sid Luckman, Adrian Burk, George Blanda and Y. A. Tittle, names that were synonymous with the passing game. Joe Kapp? His passes wobbled sometimes and floated other times, and most of the time he got to play because of his bullish way of driving a football team downfield. He made a career out of threatening to run, then dropping off dinky passes to wide-open receivers. He was more adapted to the Canadian Football League style of play, which he had spent most of his professional career doing.

The ex-California star left the Canadian League for the NFL when he was 29 years old. He seemed ideal for frigid Minnesota. Yet the Viking fans, hungry for a winner, were cool to him. For much of 1967 and 1968, he played amidst the boos of his own "followers." In 1968, he threw only 10 TD passes all year.

Joe Kapp sat on the bench at the start of the 1969 season. He got to play in game No. 2 against the defending NFL champion Baltimore Colts only because the Vikings were displeased with their quarterbacking and as usual returned to gutsy Injun Joe, who at least was a field leader.

Injun Joe went on a rampage.

He completed his first six passes of the game. One

of those was to Dave Osborn, a back, when the game was hardly two minutes old. The Osborn pass was good for 18 yards and a touchdown. Soon after, he launched a bomb to end Gene Washington, who strode 83 yards for another TD.

In the next period, Kapp threw scoring strikes of 21 yards to wide receiver Bob Grim and 13 to tight end Kent Kramer.

Then in the third quarter, he iced the game away with TD throws to Washington again, for 41 yards, and another tight end, John Beasley, for 1 yard.

Finally in the fourth quarter, he found yet another receiver for his seventh and record-tying touchdown—running back Dale Lindsey. Kapp got off a 15-yarder to him to bring the final score to 52-14, Vikings. It was the second worst defeat in the Colts' glorious history.

Ironically, one of the men whose record Kapp tied was in the crowd that day. In fact, Adrian Burk had the best "seat" in the house. He was the official backfield judge.

All in all, Kapp struck for 449 yards that day, another Viking record. And he did it in his usual maverick fashion—hitting 12 different receivers for what may be another record.

Despite his record start, Kapp did not finish among the league's top passers that season. Again, he was only tenth. But when the Super Bowl arrived, there was ol' Injun Joe, somehow completing his passes against the Kansas City Chiefs.

And from his record-tying day, no one else has ever thrown for seven TD's.

Super Bowl records didn't compare with season records until Phil Simms of the Giants outperformed every quarterback.

A Super Performance

The Super Bowl was in its 21st year in 1987, and, while the players in the first 20 of those games had set some pretty good Super Bowl records, the marks didn't compare well with regular-season game records, which had been set over seven decades.

But to Super Bowl XXI came Phil Simms, quarterback for the New York Giants, passing the football unlike almost any quarterback in the thousands of pro football games that preceded him.

When the game came to an end, with the elated Simms being named the Super Bowl's most valuable player, the 30-year-old quarterback had completed 22 of 25 passes, or 88 percent of his attempts.

Sportswriters and broadcasters were quick to point out that that percentage was the best ever in any kind of a playoff game—a whopping 15.5 percent better than the record set by Ken Anderson of the Cincinnati Bengals in the 1982 Super Bowl.

But another look at the record book makes Simms' performance even more outstanding. In the history of professional football, only two passers who threw a minimum 20 in a game had a better one-game percentage. Anderson of Cincinnati had a 90.91 percentage in a 1974 game and Lynn Dickey of the Green Bay Packers had a 90.48 percentage for a 1981 game.

After the Giants beat the Denver Broncos, 39-20, for the Super Bowl title, Ron Erhardt, the offensive coordinator for the New York team, called Simms' game "perfect."

To which the quarterback replied, "It was close."

For Phil Simms to be perfect, or even close to perfect, seemed an impossible task for most of his professional career. He had been the verbal target of Giants fans from the time he joined the team as No. 1 draft choice from little-known Morehead State in Kentucky. In fact, it was on draft day in 1979 that he first drew some boos from Giants fans. They would have preferred a better-known player.

But the Giant management felt differently. The front office—from general manager to the coaching staff—was new and wanted to build the team from scratch. They felt it best to begin at quarterback, the heart of any pro team.

George Young, the general manager who made the decision to take Simms, felt that the boyish-looking blond had the potential, and the Giants had the time. Young figured that it might take five years to find out, but that Simms was a future National Football League star. Besides, Young was not discovering some unknown quantity: about two-thirds of the teams in the league had given Simms a tryout.

But Young and his quarterback protege found out that time would be needed. Simms played as a rookie in 1979, but then suffered a series of injuries—a separated shoulder in 1980, a similar injury in 1981, knee surgery in 1982, a fractured thumb in 1983.

The fans were becoming impatient, and weary of the defeats. Simms was one of their prime targets. No wonder. The team had fallen into last place, and the offense had come to a standstill.

There was hope in 1984, when Simms got to play a full season and the Giants made the playoffs, albeit barely. And there was improvement in 1985. But Simms didn't get to share much of the glory. The critics credited the Giants with better defense, better running, better coaching. If only they had a quarterback.

The 1986 season was one of promise, with the Giants right up in contention from the start. The defense was great, the running game was clicking, the passing game—well—adequate. The Giants started out by winning 10 of their first 12 games. But there still was a smattering of boos when the passing game plodded, especially when Simms threw off target or the team chose to run instead of pass on important down after important down.

But on an early December night in San Francisco, Simms clicked in an important game against the 49ers. It was Monday night, national television, and he made all the right moves to help the Giants come from 17 points behind to win. He didn't stop for the rest of the season.

In the Super Bowl, the Giants were solid favorites because of their defense. But they had played the Broncos earlier in the season, and though they won, they didn't show much offense.

In this rematch, with so much at stake, Giants' Coach Bill Parcells put his faith squarely in the hands of Simms. The Giants made up their minds that they would go right at the Broncos with Simms. They had figured the Broncos would be geared to stopping Joe Morris, the running back who had carried the team all season long.

"I knew we were going to start out being aggressive, trying to throw the ball," Simms would recall later. "I wanted a chance to be a factor in the game. I thought that was important."

Simms' first pass was to his wide receiver, Lionel Manuel, and it was good for 17 yards and a first down. Before the period had ended, he completed six more passes without a miss, including another 17-yarder, an 18-yarder and a 6-yard touchdown pass. He threw eight more passes in the second quarter, completing five and seeing two others nearly caught.

But the Giants were behind, 10-9, at halftime, so Simms got the call again in the second half to be aggressive.

Simms was just that. In the third period, he completed all eight of his passes, five for first downs and another for a touchdown. One of the completions came on a flea-flicker play in which the running back Morris takes the handoff and after a couple of steps laterals the ball back to Simms. That came late in the third quarter with the Giants winning, 19-10. Simms then passed to Phil McConkey, a wide receiver, who was in the open, and McConkey went all the way to the 1-yard line on the 44-yard play. The Giants scored on the next play and were never in danger after that.

At the time, Simms thought, "That's it, we've won it."

With a solid lead, the Giants sat tight for most of the final period, and Simms threw only two more passes. He completed both.

To break records, one needs some luck, too.

Simms' last completion was intended for his tight end. The quarterback threw it too hard and it bounced off the end's hands and helmet. But McConkey was there when the ball came down, and Simms not only had another pass completion but another touchdown pass—his third of the day.

In summation, he finished 22 for 25, gaining 268 yards. Maybe just as important as the record was that 10 of his passes were for first downs and three others for touchdowns.

"This dispelled for the last time any myth about Phil Simms," his coach said right after the game. "He was absolutely magnificent today."

18 Passes Caught
in One NFL Game

There was no question that Tom Fears was going to be a star the moment he came into the National Football League in 1948. That season, the UCLA grad caught 51 passes for the Los Angeles Rams to lead the league. In the ensuing years, Fears would have a lot of teammates helping him—two standout quarterbacks in Bob Waterfield and Norm Van Brocklin and a dazzling receiving mate, Elroy (Crazylegs) Hirsch, to take the pressure off him. Fears made the best of his opportunities.

For three straight seasons, he led the NFL in receptions. As a second-year man he made 77 catches, to break the pro record set by the immortal Don Hutson of Green Bay. Fears may not have set the world afire after he caught the ball, especially in comparison to Crazylegs Hirsch, but he did his job and helped the Rams achieve their victories in some of their most glorious years.

As a third-year man in 1950, Fears again had a chance to lead the league as the team prepared for its final game. In fact, with 66 catches going into the December 3 game with Green Bay, he had an outside chance of matching his own league record of 77.

The Rams had the divisional title wrapped up at the time, so they could afford to play around with their potential recordbreakers. Waterfield would work the first and final quarters and Van Brocklin would pitch the ball in between.

"In some cases, it is very hard for a receiver to adjust to two different quarterbacks," Fears explained about the dual-passing situation. "But in the case of Waterfield and Van Brocklin, there really was no significant problem. Both were excellent passers and it made it easy for the receiver."

Tom Fears of the Los Angeles Rams set a pass-catching record in 1950 that is still in the record book.

As it turned out, the game became a pushover for the powerful Rams, and there would be time for Fears to get his record if he were up to the assignment.

Fears caught six passes in the first half of the game. In the third period he caught two more. The Rams rallied behind him for the fourth period. He needed three more to tie and four to break his mark.

As Fears recalled, "The guys knew I had a big day going so they sort of fed me the ball in the final quarter. There was nothing to be lost by it and the passes to me continued to click." Not only did Fears get his four, but the 6' 3", 215-pound tight end started cutting to the middle of the defense behind the line and grabbed several quick passes. He had more than enough for the record. From there, he began going through his usual mixture of patterns, and Waterfield continued to find him.

The Rams won the game, 51-14. Fears caught 10 passes in the fourth quarter alone, bringing his total for the day to 18—four over the NFL record for a single game. He also had upped his season mark to 84, a record which stood for 14 years.

When Opportunity Knocked, He Caught Passes for 309 Yards

It wasn't supposed to be much of a game—two teams going nowhere in the final game of a fruitless season for both. Only 18,178 fans showed up at Arrowhead Stadium in Kansas City, Missouri, for the National Football League season-ending game between the Kansas City Chiefs and the San Diego Chargers on December 22, 1985. Which meant nearly 60,000 seats were empty.

And the man who would make pro football history didn't seem to be going anywhere too fast either, despite a fast pair of legs.

Stephone Paige had signed with the Chiefs three seasons before as a free-agent receiver, but had yet to catch his 100th pass in the league. He was a confident young man who came through when the Chiefs needed him, but he didn't always get the chance.

Statistics show that on more than 80 percent of the occasions when the Chiefs threw to him on important third-down plays, he either made a first down or a touchdown. But the Chiefs seemed to use him as a designated third-down player, as half his catches were made under those circumstances. They just didn't seem to want to give him an opportunity to be a starter.

This was beginning to get to him, as he would recall later.

"Every time I get a chance to touch the ball I make something happen," he said. "That's a fact. If I can make the plays on third down, why can't I make them on first down? It's time to turn me loose. I've been ready for a couple of years now, but they've held me back. Maybe the coaches didn't think I was ready."

With injuries a factor, Paige did get a chance in the 1985 season finale.

Going into the game, he had not yet caught passes for 100 yards or more in a single pro game (though he had had a 246-yard day in his career-ending game at Fresno State University).

Playing wide receiver instead of his usual place in the slot position between tight end and the flanker, Paige got his 100 yards in the first quarter alone, making catches for 56 and 51 yards, including a touchdown.

In the second quarter, he teamed with quarterback Bill Kenney for plays of 30, 17, 84 and 20 yards, with the 84-yarder going all the way. That not only gave him two and a half times as much yardage as he ever had in a game, but he made six catches, one more than his best pro day ever.

His 258 yards at halftime had broken the team record for a whole game, 213 set by Curtis McClinton two decades before.

But there was a bigger record to shoot for, and it had stood for 40 years. In 1945, a wide receiver for the Cleveland Rams, Jim Benton, had caught passes for 303 yards. Nobody had come close to 300 yards since Cloyce Box of the Detroit Lions flirted with Benton's record by getting 302 yards in 1950. Pass defenses had become just too sophisticated.

But Paige was having some problems. He had hurt his ribs in the second quarter and had to come out of the game.

"My ribs hurt bad," he recalled, "it was a matter of whether I wanted to finish. My will and pride are why I went back out. I wanted to end the season on a high note and not let anything stop me."

Another motive spurred him on, too.

"When I found out I had a shot at the record, it helped some of the pain go away," he said.

Late in the third period, Kenney hit Paige with a 39-yarder that set up a field goal and gave the Chiefs a commanding 38-13 lead. That put Paige within 6 yards of Benton's ancient mark.

But the Chargers did not make it easy to get that final yardage. They began a comeback and kept holding the ball for the rest of the third quarter and most of the fourth as they scored a couple of touchdowns.

Paige began to get worried.

"The thing that rings in my mind most was that I didn't think I was going to get it," Paige recalled. "The defense was out there, the Chargers had the ball and time was running out. It was a matter of: *Would* we get it back?"

Finally the Chiefs recovered an onside kick with about five minutes to play. Kenney made up his mind he was going to get Paige the record "if I had to throw the ball to him five straight times."

It certainly didn't take that much determination.

The sure-handed Paige grabbed Kenney's first pass, a quick-out for 12 yards that brought the receiver's game total to 309, six better than the record.

Looking back on his big day, the 6-foot 2-inch, 191-pound receiver, ever the optimist, said:

"The way my day was going, I could have had 400 yards. I was that fired up. If I got 300 yards, why couldn't I get 400? It would only have been two or three more catches. I left the game in the second quarter and I still had 200-and-some odd yards. If I had played the whole first half, the way I was going, who knows?"

Who does know? But Paige got 309, and that was a pretty good fact in his favor the next year when the Chiefs put together their lineup.

10 TD Passes in a College Game

October 12, 1968 was homecoming for little North Park College in Chicago, and the theme was "Success in '68." Since 1968 was in its final quarter there wasn't too much time left to achieve the success, so quarterback Bruce Swanson took matters into his own hands.

Swanson, who happened to be engaged to the homecoming queen, got the game versus North Central College off to a rousing start by spiraling a 59-yard touchdown pass to end Paul Zaeske on the first play of the game from scrimmage. The crowd of about 3,000 partisans at North Park Athletic Field was in ecstasy. But that was only the beginning.

The collegiate record for touchdown passes in a game (a *whole* game) was eight. Swanson threw for that many in the first half alone. The fact that North Park was overwhelming its downtrodden opponent by halftime, having scored on ten of its 20 offensive plays, meant that Swanson would be limited in playing time for the second half. As it turned out, he got into the game for only five more plays. But he made the best of it, throwing for two more TDs to boost his all-time single-game college record to ten.

In order, Swanson's scoring passes were for distances of 59, 5, 31, 20, 6, 32, 6, 10, 34 and 6 yards. In all, he completed 20 of 29 passes for 345 yards.

A feat even more incredible than Swanson's TD pitches was that seven of his eight TD catches were made by his receiver Paul Zaeske, who later played in the National Football League. One more scoring reception came from Swanson's substitute to Zaeske.

The final score of the game was 104-32, giving North Park another NCAA college-division record for points in a game.

Football never saw such a one-game passing explosion than the one Bruce Swanson (12) put on with his North Park College teammates in 1968.

In all, North Park set 18 school records that day, thanks mostly to the quick hand of Swanson. But he was no newcomer to the record book. The year before, he was quick-footed, too, setting an NCAA small-college record with his 46.3-yard punting average.

Almost 10 Yards Every Carry

Beattie Feathers was as light-footed a runner as his last name suggests. He entered the National Football League in 1934, just two seasons after the league began keeping statistical records, and he put together a portfolio that the pros are still using as a yardstick in comparing the great runners. The 25-year-old rookie, fresh out of the University of Tennessee, is credited with a 9.94-yards-per-carry average that season. No one has come within 3 yards per carry of that mark.

The 5' 11", 188-pound speedster was groomed to be Red Grange's replacement with the Chicago Bears that season. After a couple of games, Grange himself became Feathers' greatest booster.

In his first game, against the Green Bay Packers, Feathers made a credible showing, as he gained 41 yards in eight carries. But after that opener, his performances were incredible. Week after week, Feathers was ripping off yardage at almost 10 yards a try. He gained 140 in his second outing at Cincinnati, 132 at Brooklyn, 101 at Pittsburgh and so on.

After 11 games, Feathers' ledger show 1,004 yards, something no pro before him had done. The he got injured and missed the last two games of the Bears' unbeaten season.

The National Football League, in tallying up Feathers' yardage, counted 101 attempts from scrimmage, divided 101 into his 1,004 yards, which gave him his 9.94-yard average. However, the Pro Football Hall of Fame at Canton, Ohio, has since reported that research in sketchy game stories indicate that Feathers lugged the ball 117 times, which would give him an 8.58 average. Whatever the figure, it's still well above the

Beattie Feathers set an NFL rushing record more than a half-century ago that has never been challenged, much less broken.

runnerup record of 6.87 yards set in 1972 by Bear quarterback Bobby Douglass.

Feathers, a popular man who later coached at Wake Forest, always cited good blocking for his 1934 feat. "I played behind the greatest blocker ever, Bronko Nagurski," he told banquet audiences who asked about his stellar performance.

Strangely enough, Feathers never gained a total of 1,000 yards in all the pro games he played in the next six years. And his per-carry average was never more than 5.0 a try. But for one season, he was as good as one could be.

Feathers' Statistics in 1934

	Attempts*	Yards	Longest Run
at Green Bay	8	41	19
at Cincinnati	18	140	32
at Brooklyn	14	132	29
at Pittsburgh	8	101	82
at Chicago Cards	15	97	27
Cincinnati	7	114	34
Green Bay	15	155	31
New York Giants	8	55	21
at Boston	11	80	24
at N.Y. Giants	10	47	12
Chicago Cards	3	42	20
at Detroit		(injured)	
Detroit		(injured)	
Totals	117*	1,004	82

(*According to the Pro Football Hall of Fame; NFL credits Feathers with 101 attempts.)

Quarterback Rushed 38 Times in One Game

With recent vintage rushers like Jimmy Brown and O. J. Simpson on the scene, no ball-carrying records could be regarded as sacred. Their names saturate the all-time lists. But there were 60 minutes back in 1934 when a quarterback had his fun carrying the ball, too.

On November 11 of that year, Harry Newman's New York Giants team was locked in a tight battle with the Green Bay Packers before an Armistice (Veterans') Day crowd of 27,000. The score was 3-3 at the half, and Packer coach Curley Lambeau was living up to his pre-game boast that his team would give the championship-bound Giants "plenty of exercise."

The person who got the biggest workout was Newman.

In the first half, Newman took a lateral from halfback Ken Strong, who started the play on his own 5. Newman zigzagged most of the way downfield before ferrying the ball to another Giant, Red Badgro, who carried the ball into the end zone. However, officials ruled that Newman had stepped out of bounds.

In the second half, Newman began taking matters into his own hands. Injuries and other problems were plaguing his backfield mates, so he began carrying the ball himself.

After playing like an iron man as he rushed over and over, Newman cut inside left tackle for a 12-yard gain, then bulled past five Packers to get into the end zone. Newman carried for 50 of the Giants' 58 yards on that drive.

Later in the third period, Newman was at it again, thrusting forward 11 yards to the Packer 3-yard line

As a New York Giant quarterback in the 1930s, Harry Newman in one game showed that passing was not his only talent.

after a fumble. From there, Newman plowed into the end zone again.

In the final period, Newman helped his teammates eat up the clock and maintain field position with more and more quarterback runs. He also found enough energy to dodge past three Packers and nail Clark Hinkle for a touchdown-saving tackle.

When they added up the statistics for that game, which the Giants won, 17-3, Newman was credited with a record 38 carries. Though his total yardage was only 117, he had established a mark for rushing attempts that would remain for almost four decades.

*   *   *

It took a busy running back, O. J. Simpson, to finally break Newman's record, with 39 carries in a game in 1973. Since then, a handful of backs have rushed more than 40 times in a game, with the record shared at 43 by Butch Woolfolk, then of the New York Giants in 1983, and James Wilder of the Tampa Bay Buccaneers in an overtime game in 1984.

But none of them were quarterbacks, as Newman was.

First to Top 2,000 Yards Rushing

As a teenager, O. J. Simpson once met Jimmy Brown, the famous No. 32 of the Cleveland Browns, when the pro football star was visiting Simpson's neighborhood in San Francisco. "You ain't so tough," O. J. told him. "I'll break your record some day."

It was a brash statement; Jimmy Brown was universally regarded as the best running back in the game at the time—if not the best in pro football history. When Jimmy Brown set records, they were supposed to stay put. For eight of his nine years as a pro, Brown led the NFL in rushing and he might have extended that accomplishment if he had not retired while at his peak. Of all of Brown's records, though, the single-season total of 1,863 yards in the rushing department seemed the most invincible.

Jimmy Brown also had the second best rushing mark for a season (1,544 yards) and the third best (1,527).

But then came O. J., sporting the same No. 32 that Brown had made famous.

The resemblance ended with the number. O. J., with his 9.3-second speed in the 100-yard dash, was more of a Gale Sayers type, only bigger. Brown was bullish although he too had good speed. Brown was more of a fullback, Simpson a halfback.

Simpson's fancy stepping style was misleading, according to the man who did the stepping. "I may not always look it," he said in 1973, "but I'm aggressive. You have to be to be a good football player, or a good anything."

In 1973 Simpson was as good a football player as ever lived. After years on the brink of real stardom with the downtrodden Buffalo Bills, Simpson was given a supporting cast of blockers who could fortify his breakaway

O.J. Simpson broke a rushing record set by his hero, Jimmy Brown, and broke a barrier at the same time.

talents. The Bills had been drafting top collegians for years to bolster their offensive line.

Simpson made good use of his help.

Beginning with a record 250-yard outburst in his opening game against the New England Patriots, Simpson startled the football world. And some opposing coaches: "It was like a track meet out there," said the Patriots' Coach Chuck Fairbanks. "O. J. looked like Grant going through Richmond."

O. J.'s 200-yard-plus game was only the 20th in football history. But after continuing the season at an unbelievable pace, Simpson finished with two more 200-yard days. In the end, the new No. 32 made Brown's records look merely mortal.

Simpson's Records in 1973

Yards rushing, one game—250, vs. New England; previous record, 247, by Willie Ellison, Los Angeles, 1971.

Yards rushing, one season—2,003; previous record, 1,863, by Jimmy Brown, 1963.

Most games of 100 or more yards, one season—10; previous record, 9, by Jimmy Brown, 1963.

Most attempts rushing, one game—39, vs. Kansas City; previous record, 38, by Harry Newman, New York Giants, 1934, and Jim Nance, Boston, 1966.

Most attempts rushing, one season—332; previous record, 305, by Jimmy Brown, Cleveland, 1963.

• III •

Just for Kicks

NFL Field-Goal Record
on His First Try

After Tom Dempsey of the New Orleans Saints catapulted a 63-yard field goal in 1970 to wipe out Bert Rechichar's 17-year-old National Football League record, Rechichar was one of the first people to offer his congratulations. "I was glad to see him do it," said Rechichar, who by then had retired from football and was back home in Bell Vernon, Pennsylvania. "Tom has accomplished a great feat. Besides, he has that bad foot and a withered hand. I'm glad someone like him was able to do it."

Dempsey had been born with physical handicaps, yet he courageously made it to pro football despite the problems. But Dempsey, who kicked regularly in the pros, was one of the modern day "specialists"—the players who command good salaries for just kicking the football.

Rechichar had come into the league as an all-around player, and mostly as a defensive back. At the University of Tennessee, Rechichar had been a standout. Among his many feats at Knoxville, he had booted a 47-yard field goal against Vanderbilt, as well as four other three-pointers. But he was drafted by the Cleveland Browns in 1952, and that team just happened to have a kicker named Lou (The Toe) Groza, who headed the pro football placement kickers for many years. Rechichar wasn't in demand as a defensive back either by the championship Brown teams. So he was traded to the Baltimore Colts the following spring.

Again Rechichar found himself being upstaged as a kicker—this time by ex-Oklahoma star Buck McPhail. Rechichar did make the Colts as a defensive back, though.

Then on September 27, 1953, with the Colts playing the defensive-minded Chicago Bears, McPhail was ready to try a field goal with only seconds remaining on the first-half clock. For some reason, though, Coach Weeb Ewbank of the Colts had a hunch that Rechichar would kick the ball further than McPhail in case he missed and would prevent the Bears from getting in field position to score.

With three seconds to go, Rechichar was asked if he could give it a try. He had already removed his helmet and was on his way to the dressing room. He muttered something to the effect, "Aw, what the heck, why not," and went into the game. He told his holder Tom Keene to place the ball down quickly, because he would need all the time he could get.

Then Rechichar slammed his foot into the ball for the first time in a pro game. It traveled 56 yards and cleared the uprights, much to the surprise of the kicker himself.

Rechichar had broken Lou Groza's distance record!

The rugged defensive back would be called upon for other long-distance kicks in the future and would respond with 54- and 53-yarders. But nothing was better than the first one, in terms of distance or incredibility.

Averaged 52.7-Yard Punts
Same Day as 46-Yard Field Goal

The year 1971 was a good one for the University of Utah's Marv Bateman. While setting a national record for best punting (48.1), the rangy kicker go off 30 punts that sailed over 50 yards. In four separate games, he averaged over 50 yards as a punter.

Bateman reached his zenith, though, in an October 30 game against the University of Wyoming.

The day was near freezing but Bateman was hot. Six of his seven punts traveled 52 yards or more. The longest was 62. The average was 52.7. More important, the booming punts were not returned very far, as long punts often are. Wyoming's runback aces could only haul the seven punts back for a total of 38 yards. Bateman had 338 yards in field position on his opponents.

To top off his fine performance, Bateman skyrocketed a 46-yard field goal that was good.

Otherwise, October 30 was glum. Utah lost the game, 29-16.

The NFL's list of great success stories has to include Tom Dempsey of the New Orleans Saints who not only overcame a handicapped foot but set a kicking record that still stands.

Long Field Goal Without His Shoe On

Tom Dempsey became a national celebrity on November 8, 1970, when he lofted a 63-yard field goal over the defensive line of the Detroit Lions. It gave the New Orleans Saints a badly needed victory and it gave Dempsey the National Football League distance record by a full 7 yards. Dempsey had been crippled from birth with one size 3 foot and the other size 10½. He also had a withered arm.

But at 263 powerful pounds and a keen desire to make the pros, Dempsey became one of the league's great folk heroes. Even after he lost his job with the Saints, he showed the determination needed to make it back to the NFL. After he came back—in 1971—he led the Philadelphia Eagles and the NFL in percentage with 12 of 17.

Like many field-goal kickers, Dempsey did some of his most amazing feats in practice, kicking 65 yarders at random.

He once made a field goal in a semipro game, though, that must rank alongside his NFL record boot in interest. After he got out of Palomar Junior College, he played on a weekend team in hopes of catching on with a regular pro team. In one of those semi-pro games, he kicked a 57-yarder—without a shoe.

17 Field Goals
in a College Freshman Game

The fans at the Montana State–Billings Tech freshman football game on November 1, 1924 had to figure something strange was going on when the Montana State yearling star, Frosty Peters, stopped short of a touchdown on purpose. Peters had broken away from the Billings defense and raced untouched toward the goal. But as he got within 10 yards, he halted and casually drop-kicked the ball through the uprights. His potential six-point touchdown had suddenly become a three-pointer.

The Montana State coach seemed unperturbed, however, at the tactics of his star back. Right away the crowd figured Peters had his coach's blessings.

The antics continued the next time Montana got the ball, as a pass receiver stopped short of the goal line in what clearly was a scoring situation. On the next play Peters drop-kicked his second three-pointer.

Peters wasn't so accurate for the rest of the half, but his teammates, obviously tuned in to the record-breaking strategy, did all they could to help against hapless Billings Tech. Twelve more times in the half, Peters got to try drop kicks; seven of those times he made them.

In the second half, the strange pattern continued, with Montana State more interested in Peters' quest for a national record (a high-school player had made 15 in 1915) than it was in touchdowns.

Peters made eight of eight in little over a quarter, bringing his total to 17 of 22. With Montana State leading, 51-0, Peters left the game and the team was allowed to go on for touchdowns.

Strangely enough, the game may have cost Montana State the services of Peters. Illinois coach Bob Zuppke heard about the feat and summoned the star to the Champaign campus. Peters obliged and never played for Montana State again.

At Illinois, there was no time for such gimmicks, and Peters would never again be involved in a record-setting situation. Besides, he had to share the glory there. In his backfield in 1925 was a halfback named Red Grange, who was setting some records of his own.

Punted 98 Yards in an NFL Game

One could say that Steve O'Neal came into the National Football League with a boom during his rookie season.

As a collegian at Texas A&M, O'Neal had averaged about 42 yards per punt during his three-year varsity career. There was nothing special to earmark him for pro football stardom, though. He had had a 73-yard kick, but that came while he was a sophomore, and most punters will get off a long one sooner or later if they kick often. To the defending world champion New York Jets, he was worth a 13th-round draft choice—the 338th player taken in the 1969 talent pool.

The Jets weren't too pleased with their regular punter, Curley Johnson, and O'Neal was afforded the chance to beat him out. O'Neal had made a 38-yard kick in the College All-Star game and went on to earn himself a job even though he did not get much longer yardage than Johnson in preseason drills.

O'Neal pretty much went unnoticed in the Jets' league opener. But then again, punters usually get little attention unless they muff a kick at a crucial time. In his second game, at mile-high Denver, he would get a better opportunity to show his stuff. The rarefied air at that altitude is a kicker's delight.

The NFL record at the time of the September 21st Jet–Bronco game was 94 yards, set by a tackle named Wilbur Henry almost 46 years before. Henry played for the old Canton Bulldogs in an era when the football was shaped more like today's volleyballs and punting was an integral part of football strategy. The 6′ 3″, 185-pound O'Neal could not begin to match the 245-pound "Fats" Henry's launching power, either. The best kick with a modern football was 90 yards by Don Chandler of the

Steve O'Neal of the New York Jets boomed a punt so far that the record can only be tied, not broken.

1965 Green Bay Packers. And Bobby Scarpitto had lifted one 87 yards for Denver at Denver in 1968.

But O'Neal was more concerned with holding a job than holding a record when the Jets went to Denver. The Jets were on their own 1-yard line when O'Neal came into the game.

Standing behind his goal line, O'Neal got off the greatest punt in pro football history. He had only a 5-mph wind in his favor. But the ball sailed over 70 yards and bounded near the Denver 30-yard line, where ace kick-returner Bill Thompson tried for a running over-the-shoulder catch. Thompson missed and the ball bounced down to the 1-yard line, where it stopped. Thompson managed a 1-yard return.

Officially, the ball traveled 98 yards, from the 1 to the other 1. You can't do any better than that and keep the ball in bounds.

The punt came out of nowhere and caught the statisticians and other experts by surprise, so there was no actual measurement as to how far the ball traveled through the air. But estimates by those on the scene say it may have gone as far as 77 yards, if one counts the distance behind the goal line from where O'Neal kicked.

O'Neal's record blast did not turn out to be a "shot heard round the world"—even the football world. It got surprisingly little play in the New York papers, his toe being upstaged by Joe Namath's injured rib. And for the year, O'Neal would finish only fourth in the 13-team American Football Conference. But he left a record that would be hard to match.

*   *   *

It was late in the third quarter of a meaningless exhibition game on August 11, 1962, and the Green Bay Packers led the Dallas Cowboys, 24-7. The Cowboys' predicament was made worse when they were forced into a punting situation.

And the situation seemed even worse when Sam Baker, the team's punter, fumbled the ball. As the world champion Packers began closing in on him, Baker picked up the ball and got off the best kick he could.

Baker got a good foot into the ball. It landed and then began to roll. And roll. And roll.

All together, the punt traveled over 100 yards, into the end zone.

Officially, he got credit for an 85-yard punt, undoubtedly the longest one ever made in a pro game after a fumble.

Percentage Kicker

Of the many facets of football strategy, none has changed the look of the game in the past three decades as much as the field goal. Part of the reason is that since rules were changed in the 1960's to encourage field-goal kicking (and thus higher-scoring games), kickers just seem to get better and better.

Undoubtedly some day a better college kicker will come along to break the records of John Lee, U.C.L.A.'s standout kicker of the 1980's. But by the time Lee left U.C.L.A., he didn't leave future would-be record-breakers much margin for error.

Consider:

1. Lee made an astounding 85.9 percent of his field goals during his career (1982-85). At one point, he had missed only one of 50 field goals within the 40-yard line.

2. Lee made 79 field goals during his career, an average of 1.84 a game. As a junior in 1984, he made 29, an average of 2.64 a game.

3. On extra points, he earned 116 of 117. After his career was over, the N.C.A.A. compiled a new record: best percentage on combined extra points and field goals. Lee was the recordholder, making 93.3 percent of all of his kicks.

Lee was the prototype of the modern-era kicker. He was bigger, at 187 pounds, than many of the foreign-born kickers who got the field-goal explosion going with the soccer-style kicks. He, too, was foreign born, in South Korea, but he got his introduction to American football at an early age while attending junior high school in California.

In fact, because of his great size, the coaches at Downey High School near Los Angeles wanted to make him a noseguard, even though he went out for the team

*In an era when
place-kickers get
better and better,
John Lee of U.C.L.A.
set some kicking
standards well
beyond the expected.*

as a kicker. He booted a 50-yarder that help change the coach's mind. Lee didn't get a chance to kick much until his final two years, but he kicked 23 of 28 on his field goals and missed only two of 51 extra points.

He received a football scholarship to U.C.L.A. and was rarely stopped after that.

Not that opponents didn't try.

In a 1985 game against Washington State, Lee faced some new tactics. He had heard all sorts of things to rattle him, but the Cougars used a new twist—they shouted his Korean name, Nin Jong Lee.

It didn't break his concentration. Lee, revved up by his thoughts of being on stage with Eddie Van Halen doing the heavy metal music "Mean Street," calmly boomed a 44-yarder to quiet the Cougars.

Lee learned to master concentration. "I take it easy," he said in a 1985 interview. "I try to think that it's not a big deal, that it's not the most important thing in life.

"When I have missed in the past, it was not because I tried to kill the ball, but because I was too careful. I've gotten over that.

"The mental approach is the most important thing, and my mental approach got better."

One thing Lee didn't worry about was records.

"The only record I can be proud of is the percentage," he said. "Whoever has the most points is the guy who has had a lot of chances. I have no control over how many field goals I kick. It just depends on how often and where the offense gets stalled."

Distance of field goals didn't concern him either.

His longest in a game was 52, but he reached 66 yards in practice, just short of the collegiate record of 67 yards.

Lee made enough field goals that counted and left his mark on college football.

• IV •

Witnesses
for the Defense

Blocked a Field Goal at the Crossbar

They called him "Alley Oop" because of his unique style of catching the looping passes that quarterback Y. A. Tittle lofted to him in their days together with the San Francisco 49ers. R. C. Owens was pro football's greatest leaper. He earned that reputation after first proving it in two other sports: basketball and high jump. At the University of Idaho, Owens had once led the nation with an astonishing 27.6-per-game rebounding average, and he high jumped almost 7 feet.

It didn't take his pro football teammates long to appreciate his bounding talents. But one teammate, star place-kicker Tommy Davis, was kidding R. C. one day as they watched game films of a Detroit Lion kick narrowly clearing the crossbar on a 50-yard field goal. "You could have gotten that one, R. C.," said Davis that day in 1960. Owens agreed.

The crossbar in football is 10 feet high, the same as the rim in basketball. And R. C. had blocked enough shots and gone above the rim for enough rebounds in his time at Idaho. So he approached 49er Coach Red Hickey and asked if he could give it a try. Hickey said no.

The 6' 3", 190-pound Owens didn't give up on his dream, though.

When he was traded to the Baltimore Colts in 1962, he approached Head Coach Weeb Ewbank with the same proposition. The two figured that it was worth a try, even if only for the psychological effect it might have on a kicker. Besides, the Colts needed a deep man to run back kicks in case the field goals fell short, and R. C. was a good man in the open field.

Owens began practicing the leap to perfect his technique. He finally got to try it in a game against his old 49er teammates. Fans looked on in disbelief as R. C. lined up underneath the goal post. But the kick fell short and Plan B went into effect. R. C. ran the ball back from the 2 to the midfield stripe.

Later in the season, Bob Khayat of the Washington Redskins teed up the ball on the 40 for a fairly long attempt and R. C. again meandered in front of the crossbar like a soccer goalie. As Khayat's kick descended toward the crossbar, R. C. carefully timed his leap— and *oomph* . . . in true Alley Oop fashion tipped the ball away.

Alley Oop had proved his point.

Ironically, the game was on national television, and not too long after Owens heard from another basketball player who said he might be interested in joining a pro team as a possible goal blocker. The player's name was Wilt Chamberlain.

R.C. Owens of the Baltimore Colts made pro football history with this block of a field goal, and also forced the NFL to change a rule.

Blocked 3 Punts
in a Single Pro Game

Along with being one of the greatest passers of all time, Slingin' Sammy Baugh of the Washington Redskins also was the premier punter in pro football history. His kicking deeds are found in many places in the National Football League record book. Sammy holds the marks for best punting average in a game (minimum 4 punts) with 59.4 yards in a 1940 game; best average in a season with 51.3; and best average in a career with 44.93. He punted often in his 16 years as a professional, and once punted 14 times in a single game.

But there was a time when punter Baugh met his match on the professional field. The adversary was a rookie lineman out of the University of Tennessee named Bob Suffridge. The newcomer was no ordinary rookie. He has been considerd as an all-time All-America guard out of the days when football players had to play offense and defense.

In a late 1941 game, when neither team was going anywhere in the standings, Baugh's Washington Redskins met Suffridge's Philadelphia Eagles. That day Bob Suffridge broke through three times to block Sammy Baugh punts. Though it didn't make the record books and it didn't save the Eagles from a 20-14 defeat, Suffridge's achievement is unequalled in pro football history.

Unfortunately for the rookie, though, history affected his achievement in more ways than one that day. Bob Suffridge chose December 7, the day World War II broke out, to accomplish his unusual feat. The newspapers had little inclination to report the performance the following day.

Scored 2 TDs on Blocked Punts

The National Football League record book has hundreds of categories, more than 200 categories for individual performances alone.

On November 11, 1973, Tim Foley of the Miami Dolphins created a new subhead in the record books: "Misc. TDs, 2 in 1 game." The NFL, for all it planning, had not allowed for a man who would score twice after blocked punts in one game. Only once had a man scored two TDs that way in one season; it happened 16 years before Foley was born.

In 1973, the Dolphins were playing their intra-divisional rival, the Baltimore Colts, for the second time when Foley broke through in the opening period and blocked Bruce Lee's punt on the 18-yard line. Foley scrambled for the loose ball and got it at the 8, then simply ran it in for his first TD.

Later in the game, his teammate, linebacker Bob Matheson, got to the veteran punter on the 14-yard line and blocked his kick. This time, Foley picked up the ball on the 5 and ran it in again.

The Dolphins won the game, 44-0.

For a rugged 6′, 194-pounder who had started three years for the high-scoring Dolphins, it was an unusual way to break into the scoring columns for the first time.

4 Interception Returns for TDs

The Houston Oilers had a difficult time winning football games in the late 1960s and early 1970s. Their few successes in that time were due in part to a guy named Houston—defensive back Ken Houston.

A record nine times in his career, Ken Houston ran back interceptions for touchdowns. The last two of those scoring bursts came in a single game, against the San Diego Chargers. Like most of Houston's other runbacks after snatching balls out of the air, that too was a National Football League record.

In each of the eight games where Ken Houston intercepted passes and returned them for scores, his team avoided defeat. The first time they fought to a tie, but after that his dazzling returns spelled victories.

Ken Houston was a hit during his first season in the league (1967), which was amazing because the 6′ 3″ safetyman from Lufkin, Texas, never played in the secondary until he reached the pros. He had been a small middle linebacker in college at Prairie View A&M. But he adapted quickly and turned in one scoring runback as a rookie. That was 1967.

He continued to accumulate interceptions with regularity from then on, but in 1971 he had the year that other defensive backs merely dream of. He was only 27 at the time.

But he had the savvy of a veteran.

"You have to plan the return," he said while being honored for his triple-crown season of 1971—most TD returns in a game, in a season, and in a career. "You have to think touchdown all the way. I want to get my interceptions on the sideline and head for the middle of the field. That gets the flow started. And when it's nicely underway, when everybody on both teams is sprinting for the center of the field, that's the time to cut back. If you're lucky, you can go."

Somebody said that a man who returns four interceptions for touchdowns in a season is more than lucky, though. Most quarterbacks in the NFL would agree to that.

Averaged Over One Interception a Game in College Career

Al Brosky liked to look into a quarterback's eyes as he played defensive back for the University of Illinois in the early 1950's. Then, as the passer would release the ball, Brosky would scoot in with all his speed and daring and swipe the ball. It was a proven formula: in three years and 25 games for the Illini, Brosky intercepted a record 29 passes.

Brosky intercepted three passes in his very first college game.

At one point in his career, the 5′ 11″, 170-pounder filched passes in 15 straight games. Twice he intercepted 10 passes in a season. He was, by any standard, the best pass thief ever to play the college game.

A Chicagoan, Brosky knew what to do with the ball when he got it, too. He had several runbacks of 30 yards or more and one scoring burst of 61. In another tough game, he had two intercepts in his own end zone.

More than three decades after his career ended in 1952, no other collegian has come close to Brosky's record total, even though college players were throwing more than ever before.

Nailed 2 Pro QBs for Safeties
Within 5 Minutes

Fred Dryer of the Los Angeles Rams is known for his unusual lifestyle. A California nature lover, Dryer lives where he's at at any given moment. His home is a van. When he goes to work, he's all business, though. The Green Bay Packer quarterbacking corps found that out on October 21, 1973.

The 6′ 6″, 240-pound Rams' lineman was tearing the Packers apart to the delight of 80,558 partisans at Los Angeles Coliseum. The ransacking was so devastating that the Packers would gain only 35 yards rushing and 28 passing during the afternoon.

Dryer admittedly had an edge on the Packers. Their regular offensive tackle—the man entrusted to block Dryer—was out of action and Green Bay had to move a guard into the important position.

Dryer took advantage of the situation all day long. But in the final period, with the Packers trying desperately to pass their way back into the game, Dryer delivered the all-time insult.

With about 11 minutes to play, he put on a hard outside rush and charged toward Packer quarterback Scott Hunter who was trying to set up in the end zone. Dryer "blind-sided" him, forcing a two-point safety.

The frustrated Packers replaced Hunter with Jim Del Gaizo the next time they got the ball.

So five minutes after Dryer's first safety, he put on another hard outside rush and smacked Del Gaizo head on in the end zone, too, for another safety. It sealed a 24-7 victory for the Rams.

In the 54 years that the National Football League had been in existence, only six teams had ever scored two safeties in a single game. Only four times had the same player recorded two safeties in a whole season. Yet Dryer matched those feats within five minutes' time in one game.

The 27-year-old Dryer had already corralled another halfback in the end zone in the 1969 season. Thus he came up with another record—three safeties in a career.

Did Not Play College Football But Played 170 Straight Games as a Pro

The Dallas Cowboys were only two years old in 1962 when they signed a player who was newer to the game than they were. The Cowboys decided to give a prominent college basketball player from Utah State a chance to make their team as a free agent.

The Cowboys, who had been losing regularly, figured they had nothing further to lose by signing Cornell Green, a three-time All-Skyline Conference cager. At 6' 3" and about 200 pounds, he had the size and speed of a gridiron star even if he didn't have the experience. The Cowboys and Green matured together.

From an inconspicuous start in which he had to defend against All-Pro flanker Boyd Dowler of the World Champion Green Bay Packers, Cornell Green began writing one of the amazing records in pro football. If Green was green, his head was clear as he tackled one of the toughest transitions an athlete with no experience can make—playing cornerback against seasoned and speedy flankers. "You come into the league and everybody has it all to learn anyway, whether they know it or not," he said.

Green just happened to learn faster than others.

He earned himself a place on the Cowboy team in 1962 and never lost his job. Though he played cornerback and safety—positions where injuries are common—he lasted for 168 regular-season games in a row, plus several other playoff games, before retiring after the 1974 season.

As the Cowboys became better and better known, Green received his share of the limelight, too. Five times he made the Pro Bowl all-star team, at both cornerback and safety. Four times he made all-pro.

Perhaps nothing showed that he learned the game better than the off-season job the Cowboys found for him: They made him a talent scout.

Recovered 4 Straight Onside Kicks

The onside kick is one of football's most interesting plays. The team that kicks off, whether to start a half or put the ball back in play after a touchdown or field goal, needs only to boot the ball 10 yards to make it a free ball. If the kickoff man can squibble the ball just over the line, it enables his teammates to dash 10 yards or so and try to recover it. The strategy is a good one for the team that's behind.

There is one problem with the onside kick strategy, however. It usually doesn't work.

But on one Saturday afternoon in 1972, the strategy worked perfectly.

Tiny Catawba College of Salisbury, North Carolina, was losing 33-0 to Carson-Newman College of Jefferson City, Tennessee, so Catawba had nothing to lose in the second half, despite the odds.

Catawba put some of its best ballhawks up front on the kickoff, and sure enough they recovered the ball. Before Carson-Newman could get over the shock, Catawba players recovered three more in a row. With each recovery, Catawba marched down the field to score. The steals enabled Catawba to control the football for 26 consecutive plays and a total of nearly 15 minutes. Before the contest was over, Catawba recovered a fifth onside kick.

The results of the strange turn of events almost resulted in a turnabout of the score. Somehow Carson-Newman hung in for a 40-34 triumph, though.

• V •

Team Efforts

73-0 Bears

Quarterback Sammy Baugh of the Washington Redskins had played enough football in his lifetime to know a "whupping" when he saw one. After his team went down to defeat to the Chicago Bears in the 1940 National Football League championship game, Baugh was asked what would have happened if the Redskins had scored first. His answer was simple and direct: "We would have lost 73-7."

Never in pro football history had one team lambasted another so badly as the Bears did the Redskins in 1940. Though it was a day of infamy in the nation's capital, at least the Redskins took the defeat realistically.

The Skins had beaten the Bears, 7-3, three weeks earlier that season, so a tight playoff game was expected. The Washington team went into the December 8 contest with a 9-2-0 record and the Chicago eleven with 8-3-0, so the matchup couldn't have seemed closer. But pre-game prognostications were as close as the Redskins

The star, Sid Luckman (left) and George Halas (right) the mastermind of the 1940s Chicago Bears' astounding championship team. They set all sorts of records and Halas set a record himself for most games won by an NFL coach.

would get. This was a day for the Bears to rule, right from the start. As sports columnist Arthur Daley of the New York *Times* wrote, "This was the day the Humane Society took off."

The fact that the contest was held in Washington's

Griffith Stadium on a beautiful afternoon added to the insult.

The Bears, brilliant in their explosive T-formation offense, zipped downfield to score 56 seconds after the opening kickoff, as fullback Bill Osmanski dashed 68 yards. Before the quarter was over, Chicago had a 21-0 lead. The Bears scored again in the second period and from then on the only contest was between the Chicago offense and the Chicago defense. Coach George Halas played all 33 of his men; 15 of them figured in the final scoring.

Some 36,000 Washington fans sat silently through the footraces to the goal line by Chicago players.

In the second half, the Chicago defense began grabbing its share of the glory as the Redskins began to play catch-up football. Touchdown No. 5 came after Baugh intended a pass for one of his receivers deep in his own territory. The Bears' Hampton Pool swiped it out of the air and ran it back for a TD. After the sixth Bear TD, the Bears' George McAfee stole a pass and carried it 34 yards to the end zone. Later, Bulldog Turner returned a 21-yard interception to score. The Bears scored again, and then again as Turner fell on a fumble on the 2-yard line to set up the Bears' tenth touchdown. By now the Bears had surpassed the NFL scoring record with their 67th point.

After that, there was another interception which touched off a scoring drive. The Bears drove again and made the score 73-0.

Once during the game the Redskins drove to the Bears' 6-inch line. Appropriately the drive stalled there.

It was hardly a game, much less a contest, but the Bears' George Halas, who fashioned 325 victories in his pro coaching career, said he felt it was a pivotal game in football history. For one thing, he analyzed, it touched off the era of the T-formation; "People who never used the T before put it in immediately," he said. "They didn't use anything else for the rest of their lives."

He added, "Since then, football hasn't been the same. The game made us a major league."

222-0 Comedy

The problems for Cumberland College of Lebanon, Tennessee began before the little school's football squad boarded the train for Atlanta to play powerful Georgia Tech on October 7, 1916. Cumberland was to be one of those early-season warmup games for Tech, which was just coming off an unbeaten campaign. But the Tennessee team began miscalculating at about the same time it accepted a $500 guarantee to go to Atlanta. For one thing, there was a problem in rounding up enough healthy bodies to compete against Yellowjackets; Cumberland's team was fairly informal. Cumberland also failed to acquire a handful of their regulars who came from nearby Vanderbilt, despite a previous, somewhat unscrupulous agreement. Finally, when the Cumberland squad was assembled for the trip, three players missed the train.

Butch McQueen, the Cumberland law student who served as the team's coach, ordered his club aboard, anyway, confident that he could match wits with Tech coach John Heisman.

At Atlanta's Grant Field, about 1,000 fans showed up, expecting to see a possible replay of the previous week's 61-0 victory of Tech over Mercer. Cumberland was that bad and Tech fans knew it.

Coach Heisman, for whom the major football trophy

is named, was a brilliant strategist. For a moment before the kickoff, however, his own fans may have disputed that fact. He ordered Tech to kick off, rather than receive, after it won the pre-game coin toss.

That decision alone gave Cumberland an opportunity to make its big rushing play of the game. After Cumberland's regular quarterback was knocked unconscious on the first play, Morris Gouger stepped in at the position and plowed into the Tech line. His 3-yard gain would become one of Cumberland's brighter moments.

During the game, Cumberland would compile a minus-45 yards rushing, partly the result of nine fumbles. Two of 11 passes would go for 14 yards.

Meanwhile, Tech started off its day by returning Cumberland's first punt to the 20 and scoring on the very next play. Cumberland dropped the ensuing kickoff and it was scooped up by a Tech player and hauled in for the second TD.

When Cumberland fell behind, 28-0, McQueen changed his strategy and decided to kick off after the Tech TDs. But that didn't work either. Before long Tech led 42-0.

Cumberland tried receiving again but couldn't move the ball, and Tech scored once more. So Cumberland tried kicking off but Tech hauled it back 90 yards for yet another TD. The quarter ended with the Yellowjackets in the lead, 63-0. Tech exactly doubled that score by halftime.

Tech didn't show any real mercy in the second half, but it did start giving the ball to people like tackles. They scored, too. In fact, Tech began to score every time it got the ball.

Cumberland's lone "drive" came on a 10-yard pass. But the play got the Tennessee school nowhere. They were at third down and 28 when the big gainer took place.

Stories have been passed down through the years as to what happened in the final minutes of this historic game. Rumor has it that Cumberland players were seen huddling on the Tech bench, hoping that their own coach could not find them and make them go back into the game. Another legend relates that a fullback, fearful of being pounced on by Tech players, refused to heed a teammate's shout to fall on a fumble. His reply: "Not me. I didn't drop it."

Tech gained 528 yards rushing that day and another 440 yards on kick returns. But the final score—222-0—is the statistic that has stood up over the years. Never before or since has a college team topped the 200 mark.

Two years later Tech was at it again. In 1918, the Yellowjackets rolled up more than 100 points against three different opponents. Cumberland wasn't one of them. The little team had had enough of the big time in 1916.

Won 78 Consecutive Games

The football seasons from 1942 through 1949 were good ones for little Bedford County Training School in Shelbyville, Tennessee. The all-black high school won 78 games in a row.

Actually, Bedford County T.S. was tougher than the streak sounds—if that is possible.

For the first three years of the streak, no opponent crossed its 50-yard line. For the first 52 games of the skein, no one scored on this remarkable team. Edward Finley coached the team to its first 75 victories, before moving on to a junior high school in Nashville, where he put together another long streak. He said his biggest margin of victory at Bedford County was 68-0.

That was unusual, however. Finley liked to get as many second- and third-stringers into the games as possible in order to have experienced players who could continue the winning streak. There were no big-name All-Americas to come out of the teams that compiled the winning streak, but Finley proudly pointed out that 21 of his former players went on to finish college after getting football scholarships.

The glories of Bedford County Training School and its all-time high-school winning streak are a thing of the past, though. The school has been renamed Harris High. The principal there in 1965, who also coached during the streak, said that his school was having trouble recapturing past fortunes. "The integration problem plagues," he said, noting that other schools have siphoned off his best athletes.

Undefeated, Untied and Unscored-On

Undefeated and untied college football teams aren't exactly a dime a dozen. Yet there is at least one every year. Undefeated, untied and unscored-on teams, however, are extinct. In the past half-century there has been only one big-time team that could claim that distinction. And with the current rules that call for longer seasons, wide-open offenses, platoon systems and more plays in a game, the likelihood of seeing another major-college football team with a perfect all-shutout record is remote.

The last team to perform the feat was Colgate, a prominent college in Hamilton, New York, that has become one of the lesser lights in big-time college football. The year was 1932.

The Colgate Red Raiders began prepping for their historical season in 1929 when they brought in a brilliant football strategist named Andy Kerr to be head coach. Appropriately his first team scored a shutout in its first game. White-washings became commonplace with Kerr-coached teams. In his first three seasons at Colgate, the Red Raiders recorded 19 of them in 29 games. Then came 1932.

That year, Kerr assembled a team that he called not physically powerful but "unsurpassed in intelligence." Kerr applied the lessons he had learned as an assistant under the fabled Glenn (Pop) Warner.

In its opener that season, Colgate rolled up 41 points on hapless St. Lawrence University and pushed the opponents all over the field on defense. For its next seven games, the Red Raiders were also as tight as the purse-strings of that Depression year. Opponents weren't even coming close to Colgate's goal line. The season finale, however, was expected to be more of a real test of Colgate's strength. Brown University was bringing in an undefeated team that was pretty good in its own right on defense. The Bruins had given up only 21 points in their first seven games.

Brown threatened to ruin Colgate's unblemished record in the first half as a Bruin back got within inches of the goal line on the final play before the intermission. But he was stymied. In the second half, Colgate's defense stiffened and the Raiders roared back to beat Brown, 21-0.

*   *   *

In the days that were to follow, Colgate added another "un" to its undefeated, untied, unscored-on record. Surely the Red Raiders would be asked to take part in a post-season bowl game—but they went "uninvited."

Perhaps getting shut out themselves—by the bowls—was a blessing for this remarkable team. In 1938, Duke University went undefeated, untied and unscored-on in the regular season, then had its record tarnished with a 7-3 defeat by Southern Cal in the Rose Bowl. In 1939, Tennessee's greatest team ever was unbeaten, untied and unscored-on, too, in the regular season, only to lose 14-0 in the Rose Bowl. Again the culprit was Southern Cal.

The 1932 Record

Colgate		Opp.
41	St. Lawrence......................	0
27	Case Tech	0
47	Niagara U.	0
35	Lafayette	0
14	New York U.	0
31	Penn State.......................	0
32	Mississippi College	0
16	Syracuse..........................	0
21	Brown............................	0

53 Pro Football Candidates
in College One Season

There's no official record for the number of players from one school who go on to professional football, but it would be difficult to top the 1947 Notre Dame squad. That year at South Bend, the Irish had gathered at least 53 players, including freshmen (who were ineligible for varsity ball) who went on to the pros. Considering the fact that there were fewer pro teams then than now, the figure is astonishing.

Just about anybody who was anybody on that great Notre Dame squad got a pro contract after he got out of college. Among the stars were three quarterbacks— All-American Johnny Lujack, backup man Frank Tripucka and freshman Bobby Williams. On the line, George Connor, the captain and star tackle, and Leon Hart, a future Heisman winner and end, would be top picks. So would All-Americas Emil Sitko, a fullback, and Bill Fischer, a guard. Jim Martin, an all-around lineman, and Jerry Groom, a center, would be among the future pro stars.

Just about the only player of note without a pro future was little halfback Terry Brennan, the team's leading game-breaker and scoring leader. He later came back to Notre Dame as head coach.

If the Irish of that vintage were prolific in providing future pros, it was no wonder. The 1947 Notre Dame team was considered the best ever in the school's sparkling history. They won all nine games, scoring 291 points to 52 for the opposition. Only Northwestern came close to the Irish at the final gun, and Notre Dame won that game by eight points. The Irish were in the midst of four straight unbeaten seasons.

Alabama Is Bowl Bound

No team in the history of college football has gone "bowl-ing" more times than the University of Alabama.

From New Year's Day, 1926, through the 1986 season, the Crimson Tide has taken part in a record 39 post-season classics. That's a half-dozen more than any other team.

Alabama has played in each of the "Big Four" of bowls—the Rose Bowl, the Cotton Bowl, the Orange Bowl and the Sugar Bowl. In fact, it was the first school to appear in all four. The first Southern team to go to the Rose Bowl, in 1926, it was the last non-Big Ten school to be the guest team there, in 1946. Each time Alabama won.

Alabama was the first team to play for the national championship in a bowl game (in 1966, after The Associated Press decided to take the bowl games into consideration before making its final tabulation of votes). It won, beating Nebraska, which had been ranked No. 1 going into the game. Alabama also holds the record for the most points in a bowl game—61 versus Syracuse in the 1953 Orange Bowl. Alabama also has the distinction of being involved in one of bowl game history's most bizarre events; in the 1954 Cotton Bowl, Alabama star Tommy Lewis jumped off the bench to tackle Rice's Dicky Moegle, who was en route to a touchdown.

But for all of its bowl achievements, nothing is more impressive than Bear Bryant's coaching feat of taking the Crimson Tide to 24 straight bowls from 1959 through 1982, shortly before he died. It broke the stretch of 14 straight bowl appearances by Ole Miss under Johnny Vaught and Bruiser Kinard. Bama beat Ole Miss in their only bowl showdown in 1964.

For all its bowl appearances, Alabama has a 22-14-3

No football coach found his way to bowl games more than Alabama's Paul (Bear) Bryant, shown here at the Gator Bowl, the last game he coached in his fabled career.

record to show for its games through 1986. Bryant was 13-10-1.

*   *   *

One football coach, Bobby Dodd of Georgia Tech, set the most enviable bowl record by winning eight straight post-season matches. No one has come close to wiping out that mark of distinction. Dodd took over as Georgia Tech coach in 1945. A year later, his 1946 team went to the now-defunct Oil Bowl and defeated St. Mary's of California, 41-19. The Yellowjackets repeated their bowl success the following year at Miami, defeating Kansas, 20-14, for the Orange Bowl title.

Georgia Tech was out of post-season games until after the 1951 season. Then the Yellowjackets came back to score triumphs in bowl games for six straight years.

Prolific Scoring Prep Teams

In 1919, Harrisburg (Pennsylvania) Tech put it all together. In its 12 games that season, Tech scored a total of 701 points, for a per-game average of 58.4.

Tech's opponents weren't so prolific. All together they scored a total of zero points.

*   *   *

For a single-game record, the slaughter that Haven (Kansas) High administered to Sylvia High in 1928 stands out. Haven won that contest with no trouble, 256-0.

During the season, Haven High poured it on a few other opponents, too. The combined scores were Haven, 578 points; Opponents, 0.

*   *   *

Undefeated, untied and unscored-on high-school elevens are found not only in the dark ages of American football. In 1973, Arthur Hill High School of Saginaw, Michigan, outscored its nine foes, 443-0.

• VI •
Extra Points

Figured in Every NFL Statistical Category

When Doak Walker left the campus of Southern Methodist University in 1950, the football world figured he had left his fabled career behind. At SMU, Walker had performed miracles week after week, passing, running and kicking the football. He was a three-time All-America and a Heisman Trophy winner. Many years later, *Life* magazine would characterize his as the "last of the genuine college football heroes" as far as campus adulation was concerned.

The pros were something else. First of all, Doak weighed little more than 170 pounds, and there were days, when, after running, passing and kicking, he would come out of a game weighing only 155. The Detroit Lions, however, figured he was worth a first-round draft choice (they had two of them that year and made Doak their second) if not just as a drawing card alone. Walker did not let the Lions down. In his first season, he led the National Football League in scoring and his point total—128—was the second highest on record at the time.

"The Doaker" was great to the end in the pros, even if he did retire somewhat prematurely after the 1955 campaign. He was all-pro halfback in four of his six seasons and led the Lions into the title game three times, two of which they won. He led the league in scoring in both his first and final seasons and he set a Lion career scoring record of 534 points.

But for all his feats in football, an obscure one in his final season may have been his most remarkable. In 1955, Doak Walker figured in all ten of the NFL's statistical categories. It was no fluke; Walker ran, passed, caught passes, place-kicked, punted, ran back kicks and intercepted a pass as part of his week-by-week chores.

The fact that he was injured often during that final year made his statistics more amazing.

Here's Walker's record for 1955:

Rushing: Ran 23 times for 95 yards (including a 51-yard TD jaunt) and two touchdowns. Averaged 4.1 yards a carry.

Passing: Attempted three and, for the first year in his career, completed none.

Receiving: Caught 22 for 428 yards (including a 70-yarder) and five touchdowns. Averaged 19.5 yards a catch.

Extra Points: Made 27 of 29.

Field Goals: Made nine of 16 (including a 41-yarder).

Pro football has been blessed with some great all-around players, but Doak Walker of the Detroit Lions managed to show his versatility statistically more than any other player.

Scoring: Had 96 points (tops in league).

Punting: Booted nine for a 40.2-yard average when Detroit's regular punter got hurt. Walker was never a regular punter in the pros.

Punt Returns: Had two for 5 yards.

Kickoff Returns: Had one for 24 yards.

Interceptions: Had one for 20 yards.

If Doak Walker's record for getting into the statistical columns endures, it will probably be because of pro football's specialized nature today. But then again the Doak Walkers don't come along with any regularity either.

Speed "King of the Hill"

There is no statistic bandied about more loosely in professional football (and colleges and high schools, too) than the unofficial statistic—a man's speed. Press books, sports pages, and the television airwaves are saturated with tales of men who have run the 40-yard dash in 4-point this and 4-point that. The figures are tossed around almost recklessly.

Unfortunately, the clockings are taken by football coaches who often do not know the intricacies of timing athletes. Furthermore, since the clockings are taken individually or among team members, there is little way of comparing the best sprinters and coming up with the fastest man.

Bob Hayes had once proved he was the "World's Fastest Human" when he won the 100-meter dash at the 1964 Olympic Games. He also was the first person to run the 100-yard dash in 9.1 seconds. But those were triumphs of his past—the Olympic victory coming in 1964 at Tokyo and the record 100 taking place in 1963 at St. Louis, Missouri. When the 1972 football season began, Hayes had reached age 30 and was believed to be far removed from speedy clockings. In fact, Hayes, who has one of the highest yards-per-catch averages in football history, was having a struggle getting playing time with the Dallas Cowboys.

There were men who challenged his claim to "World's Fastest Football Human." Cliff Branch of the Oakland Raiders, Mel Gray of the St. Louis Cardinals, Earl McCullouch of the Detroit Lions and Richmond Flowers of the New York Giants were among the many "flyers" who had some track and field records in their own athletic careers.

The questions about Hayes lingered because he

For pure speed, no NFL player could move like Bob Hayes, on a football field or on a running track.

seemed to be on the downcurve of his career, ranking only fifth among receivers on his own team. His 13.3-yard-per-catch statistic was almost 7 yards off his lifetime average.

The off-season gave Hayes a chance to redeem himself, though.

In an effort to attract fans from other sports, the new International Track Association added what it called a "King of the Hill" event to its pro track tour in early 1973. Hayes, who always maintained a love for the sport that first brought him national acclaim, was quick to sign up.

A man who lost only twice in the short sprints a decade before, Hayes showed the old zest on the tour after losing in his debut to Cliff Branch. Both men sped to 4.5-second clockings, but Branch beat Hayes by a nose.

After that there was no stopping "Bullet Bob." He began winning week after week until he collected first-place prizes in all 14 of the remaining sprints on the pro tour. When 9.2 sprinters like Branch and Gray pushed him, Hayes accelerated. In one of those situations, Hayes ran a 4.3 40—for a pro track record. The timers were legitimate, unlike the pro football coaches. And Bob Hayes again was the unquestioned "King of the Hill."

Good as Gold

Bob Hayes was not the only man to wear an Olympic gold medal and a National Football League uniform. The pros have coveted speed-burners.

Here is a list of those players, including Hayes, who went to play in the National Football League after first winning gold medals in the Olympics:

Jim Thorpe, 1912 decathlon and pentathlon winner. Back with several teams before and after the advent of the league in 1919.

Jim Bausch, 1932 decathlon. Back, Cincinnati Reds and Chicago Cardinals, 1933.

Pete Mehringer, the only non-trackman on the list, won the 192½-pound freestyle wrestling title in 1932. Tackle, Chicago Cardinals, 1934-36.

Milt Campbell, 1956 decathlon. Back, Cleveland Browns, 1957.

Glenn Davis, 1956 and 1960 400-meter hurdles and 1960 1,600-meter relay. Receiver, Detroit Lions, 1960-61, though he never played in college at Ohio State.

Henry Carr, 1964 200 meters. Defensive back, New York Giants, 1965-67.

Bob Hayes, 1964 100 meters. Receiver, Dallas Cowboys, 1965-74, and San Francisco 49ers, 1975.

Jim Hines, 1968 100 meters and 400-meter relay. Receiver, Miami Dolphins, 1969.

Tommie Smith, 1968 200 meters. Receiver, Cincinnati Bengals, 1969.

Gerald Tinker, 1972 400-meter relay. Receiver, Atlanta Falcons, 1974-75, and Green Bay Packers, 1975.

Lam Jones, 1976 400-meter relay. Receiver, New York Jets, 1980-86.

Ron Brown, 1980 400-meter relay. Receiver and kick returner, Los Angeles Rams, 1985-86.

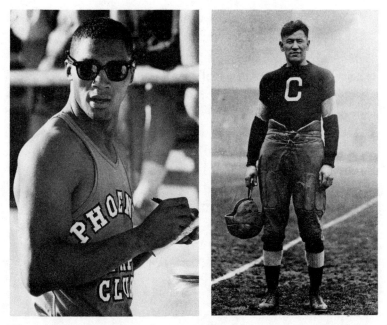

Two of the few men who earned gold medals in the Olympics and played in the National Football League: Henry Carr (left) and Jim Thorpe (right).

The Mrs. Played Pro Football

Like many minor-league professional sports franchises, the Orlando Panthers of the Atlantic Coast Football League were looking for a gimmick to spruce up the attendance for the 1970 season. The Florida team looked hard—but not far. The Panthers decided to utilize a woman player in their August 15 game with Bridgeport, Connecticut. Their candidate for the manly chore was 27-year-old housewife Pat Palinkas, whose husband just happened to be the Panther place-kicker.

Pat had held the football on the kicking tee in the past while her husband practiced, so the Panthers were not exactly introducing the game to a neophyte. The team announced that she would enter the roster and would hold for her husband.

Funny, right?

Well, one of the Bridgeport players didn't think so.

As Pat lined up the ball after the Panthers' first touchdown, in swooped defensive lineman Wally Florence, who had been trying to eke out a living in football after starring at Purdue University seven years before.

When Pat fumbled the center's passback, the 235-pound Florence crushed her into the ground, soiling her brand-new No. 3 jersey. At 5' 6" and 122 pounds, Pat was at once both the smallest and sorriest player in pro football.

Pat held for two more kicks, which were good as the Panthers won, 26-7.

If Pat was sore, Florence wasn't sorry.

After the game, he told newsmen who had gathered for the historic event: "I tried to break her neck. I don't know what she's trying to prove. I'm out here trying to

Pat Palinkas only had to walk onto a pro football field to make history: as a place-kick holder she was the first and only woman ever to play in a men's pro football game.

make a living and she's out here prancing around, making a folly out of a man's game."

End quote.

And nearly the end of Pat Palinkas' career. She retired shortly thereafter.

A Full 60 Minutes
in 3 Consecutive Rose Bowls

Modern football players may be durable, but the two-platoon system and emphasis on specialists don't allow them to be tested for their staying power under game conditions. But even if they were given the opportunity, it is doubtful that anyone would ever match the record established in the mid-1930s by Stanford University tackle Bob Reynolds.

On January 1, 1934, Reynolds played the full 60 minutes in the Rose Bowl against Columbia. It's difficult to pin down what the 6' 4", 220-pounder from Okmulgee, Oklahoma, did, but he must have been pinning down somebody on defense. The Stanford Indians held Columbia to 77 yards and just five first downs rushing. Still, Stanford lost, 7-0.

The next New Year's Day, Stanford again was in the Rose Bowl, this time against the famous Alabama team that featured Don Hutson. Thanks to Reynolds going both ways again for the full 60 minutes, Stanford got the best of the Crimson Tide in the running game. But Hutson had a field day on passes. Stanford went down again, this time 29-13.

Out West, many fans were cheering for Stanford to make it to the Rose Bowl again in 1936. It would give the famed "Vow Boy" team a chance for revenge and the All-America left tackle an opportunity to set a record that might be matched but could never be beaten—that of playing three straight 60-minute Rose Bowl games.

The Indians had a banner season, limiting their opponents to only 13 points, and were the natural choice to represent the West Coast in the 1936 Rose Bowl. Led by Reynolds in the game against Southern Methodist's

For ironman performances, Bob Reynolds of Stanford University set a bowl record which hasn't been approached.

national champions, the Indians held the Mustangs to a mere 40 yards on the ground. Reynolds played his 60 minutes again as Stanford won, 7-0. Wrote Braven Dyer of the Los Angeles *Times*, "It is questionable if there is a better tackle in the country than Bob Reynolds was this day."

In later years, Reynolds' name would be linked to sports again. As owner of several West Coast radio stations, the former Stanford tackle helped start the California (née Los Angeles) Angels baseball franchise.

Seven Brothers Played
for Same Old-Time Pro Team

Nepotism hardly has a place on the football field, where men have to make it on their own. There have been brothers on major-college teams but usually two, not seven. Yet one of football's first professional teams featured seven brothers, as well as the son of one of the brothers.

The team was called the Columbus Panhandles, not because of their financial shortcomings but because the Ohio capital was served by the Panhandle Division of the Pennsylvania Railroad. Six of the Nesser brothers formed the nucleus of the team when it was founded to play professional football in 1906.

The Nessers were a railroad family based in Columbus. One of them, young Raymond, played only briefly. But Ted, John, Phil, Al, Frank and Fred—and later Ted's son—played for years in the early days of the professional game. One of them (Al) was still active in topflight competition in 1931, when he was 38. Phil played until he was 40 and Ted and Frank until they were 37. Fred Nesser played until he was 35. None of them could match John for staying power; he quit at age 46.

Though pro football may not have been the highly organized game it is today, the Nessers played in competition that was the best offered after the turn of the century. None of the brothers or Ted's son prepped for their part-time pro careers in college football.

For the Nessers, football was no easy task. They worked in the railroad shops as mechanics until 4 o'clock each day, grabbed their meals and took off for any point within 12 hours of Columbus to play weekend games. Then they would dash back to Columbus in time to be

Family ties were never stronger in the National Football League than when the Nesser brothers teamed together. From left, Ted, John, Phil, Al, Frank and Fred.

to work at 7 A.M. Monday morning. Their uniforms proudly bore the colors of the Pennsy Railroad—gold and maroon.

Father Nesser reportedly served as the team's manager while the mother washed and mended the uniforms. Only one male member of the Nesser clan did not play football as a pro. He was 350-pound Pete.

A National Championship
in First Year as Head Coach

Bennie Oosterbaan had been good to the University of
Michigan as an athlete. During his undergraduate years
in the 1920s, he had starred in four sports. He was an
All-America in football (Grantland Rice named him to
his all-time team) and in basketball. In baseball, it was
said he could have jumped right from the campus to the
majors. In track he had Olympic potential as a discus
thrower. But Oosterbaan wanted no part of professional
athletics or the Olympics after his graduation. Instead,
he stayed at the Ann Arbor campus to become an assistant football coach.

For two decades, Oosterbaan pretty much stayed in
the background, serving three head coaches. During one
period, he doubled as the Wolverines' basketball coach,
but he was almost as undistinguished as coach there as
in football—his teams never topped the .500 mark in
nine seasons.

In 1947, under Fritz Crisler, Michigan put together
one of the greatest teams of all time. The Wolverines
went head-to-head all season long with Notre Dame in
the ratings game, switching on and off in the No. 1 spot.
The Irish won out in the final poll because they whipped
a ranked Southern Cal team, 38-7, in their last game
of the season. In those days, the wire service polls did
not include bowl results. However, after the Wolverines
crushed Southern Cal in the Rose Bowl, 49-0, the
Associated Press conducted another—unofficial—poll,
and the Wolverines were named the nation's finest team
by a 2-to-1 margin. Oosterbaan had been the backfield
coach of that 1947 "Mad Magicians" team, an aggregate
that scored 394 points in ten games. But it was Crisler,

A rookie coach, Bennie Oosterbaan, made a perfect debut as head coach at the University of Michigan.

of course, who got the publicity. The veteran head coach was named the national "Coach of the Year." After the season was over, Crisler retired to devote full time to his other position of athletic director. Oosterbaan was named Michigan's new coach for 1948.

Compared to the dynamic, innovative Crisler,

Oosterbaan was quiet and low-key. Some people described him as the "big lazy Dutchman." Some said he got his job because he was part of the university's tradition.

Oosterbaan retained only the remnants of the great 1947 team for his coaching debut. Gone were two All-America backs and most of both the offensive and defensive lines. Oosterbaan, who had been an end as a player, rose to the occasion and groomed two sophomores for his halfbacks, a reserve for his fullback and switched another back, Pete Elliott, from halfback to quarterback. He also patched up the lines.

In the opening game of the 1948 season, Michigan beat its cross-state rival, Michigan State, by a 13-7 score. If Oosterbaan was happy to get out of the game with a victory, some of his critics weren't. The year before, Michigan had beaten the Spartans, 55-0. Oosterbaan's opening day was not helped by the fact that Michigan State's coach was Biggie Munn, a former Wolverine assistant who some Michigan people had figured was Crisler's logical successor.

Michigan's youthful team began to jell, though, right after the opener. It would not become the high-scoring juggernaut of the previous year, but as the season wore on, the offensive unit began averaging about three touchdowns a game and the defense contributed five shutouts. Week after week, the Woverines got better and better and they climbed into the No. 1 spot in the polls. They clinched the No. 1 ranking by climaxing their season with a 13-3 triumph over arch-rival Ohio State. The Wolverines were a perfect 9-0-0 for their new coach.

Only once since college football began proclaiming national champions in 1924 had a man led a team to the top in his initial season as head coach of the school. And that lone exception—Matty Bell of the 1935 Southern

Methodist team—had been head coach at Texas A&M for several years before getting the SMU position.

Oosterbaan was a first-time head coach in all ways, with no coaching experience in the high school or college ranks. For his remarkable transition Bennie Oosterbaan was named "Coach of the Year." His feat has never been duplicated.

Coached Unbeaten High-School Team when Just 19 Years Old

What makes a good football coach? Experience?

Tony Versaci wanted very badly to play college football at the University of Detroit. Tony's father had once been a football hero there, so Tony gave it a try as a wide receiver and defensive back, despite the fact that he weighed only 145 pounds. But in his freshman year he injured his knee and had to give up the game—at least as a player. Not content to be a fan, he began helping out as a part-time assistant at a new school, Divine Child High, his alma mater. Divine Child was as small as the name implies, with an enrollment of about 250 boys. That was in the late 1950s.

During Tony's second year at the school, the head coach became ill two days before the opening game. It was obvious that he would have to give up the strenuous job of coaching. A petition was made to the state Board of Education, asking if a 19-year-old college undergraduate could take over the reins at a desperate school. The Board gave Versaci the go-ahead.

That season Divine Child, under its boy wonder,

went unbeaten. Was the team surprised? Well, not really. Before the season started, the teenage coach told his teenage players, "We are going to win the championship." And they did.

Versaci proved during the 1960s that his first triumph was not a one-shot affair. In his 11 years at the school, Divine Child lost only nine games. Five times they were state champions and seven times they won Detroit city titles. His little school was knocking off high schools of 6,000 enrollment before he moved on to Michigan State in 1970.

In 1971 Versaci was signed to coach the St. Louis Cardinals' specialty teams. At age 32, he did not set any record for being the youngest coach in the National Football League. But he may have been the youngest NFL coach who had never played college football.

The National Football League's One-Game Wonders

Points—40, Ernie Nevers, Chicago Cardinals, 1929

Touchdowns—6, Nevers, 1929; Dub Jones, Cleveland Browns, 1951; Gale Sayers, Chicago Bears, 1965

Extra Points—9, Pat Harder, Chicago Cardinals, 1948 and again in 1949; Bob Waterfield, Los Angeles Rams, 1950; Bob Thomas, Chicago Bears, 1980

Field Goals—7, Jim Bakken, St. Louis Cardinals, 1967

Yards Rushing—275, Walter Payton, Chicago Bears, 1977

Passes Completed—42, Richard Todd, New York Jets, 1980

Yards Passing—554, Norm Van Brocklin, Los Angeles Rams, 1951

Interception Yards—177, Charlie McNeil, San Diego Chargers, 1961

Punting Average—61.75, Bob Cifers, Detroit Lions, 1946

Punt Return Yards—207, LeRoy Irvin, Los Angeles Rams, 1981

Kickoff Return Yards—294, Wally Triplett, Detroit Lions, 1950

Quarterback Sacks—6, Fred Dean, San Francisco 49ers, 1983

Roster of Players and Teams

Roster of Players and Teams

Abilene Christian College 28
Alabama, University of 95, 96, 110
Albion College 9
Anderson, Ken 37
Arthur Hill High School 98
Atlanta Falcons 106

Badgro, Red 53
Bakken, Jim 119
Baltimore Colts 34, 35, 60, 74, 75, 77
Bateman, Marv 61
Baugh, Sammy 76, 84, 86
Bausch, Jim 106
Bears, Chicago 84-86
Beasley, John 35
Bedford County Training School (Harris High) 90
Bell, Matty 116
Bengals, Cincinnati 37, 106
Benton, Jim 45, 46
Billings Tech 64
Bills, Buffalo 56
Blanchard, Doc 30
Blanda, George 23, 24, 34
Blocking Field Goal 73
Blocking Punts 76, 77
Box, Cloyce 45
Branch, Cliff 103, 105

Brennan, Terry 94
Bridgeport 108
Broncos, Denver 37
Brosky, Al 79
Brothers 112
Brown, Jimmy 53, 56-58
Brown, Ron 106
Brown University 92
Browns, Cleveland 56, 60, 106, 119
Bruins 92
Bryant, Paul (Bear) 27, 95-97
Buccaneers, Tampa Bay 55
Buffalo 9
Buffalo Bills 56
Bulldogs, Canton 66
Burk, Adrian 34, 35

Campbell, Milt 106
Canton Bulldogs 66
Cardinals, Chicago 103, 106, 118, 119
Cardinals, St. Louis 103, 118, 119
Carr, Henry 106, 107
Carson-Newman College 83
Catawba College 83
Cedarville Yellowjackets 14, 15
Chamberlain, Wilt 74

Chandler, Don 66
Chargers, San Diego 44, 78, 119
Chicago Bears 23, 50, 60, 84-86, 119
Chicago Cardinals 106, 119
Chicago, University of 13, 14
Chiefs, Kansas City 35, 44, 46, 47
Cifers, Bob 119
Cincinnati Bengals 37, 106
Cincinnati Reds 106
Cleveland Browns 56, 60, 106, 119
Cleveland Rams 45
Coaches 114-117
Colgate Red Raiders 91-93
Colts, Baltimore 34, 35, 60, 74, 75, 77
Columbia 110
Columbus Panhandles 112
Comedy 87
Connor, George 94
Cougars, Washington State 72
Cowboys, Dallas 69, 81, 82, 103, 106
Crimson Tide 95, 110
Crisler, Fritz 114, 115
Cumberland College 87-89

Dallas Cowboys 69, 81, 82, 103, 106
Davis, Glenn 106
Davis, Tommy 73, 74

Dean, Fred 119
Del Gaizo, Jim 80
Dempsey, Tom 59, 62, 63
Denver Broncos 37
Detroit Lions 45, 63, 73, 99-101, 103, 106, 119
Detroit, University of 117
Dickey, Lynn 37
Divine Child High 117, 118
Dodd, Bobby 97
Dolphins, Miami 77, 106
Douglass, Bobby 52
Dowler, Boyd 81
Downey High School 70
Dryer, Fred 80-81
Duke University 92

Eagles, Philadelphia 28, 63, 76
Edmonton Eskimos 27
Elliott, Pete 116
Ellison, Willie 58
Elon (North Carolina) College 28
Erhardt, Ron 37
Eskimos, Edmonton 27
Ewbank, Weeb 60, 74

Fairbanks, Chuck 58
Falcons, Atlanta 106
Fears, Tom 41-43
Feathers, Beattie 50-52
Field-Goal Records 59, 61, 63, 64
Finley, Edward 90
Fischer, Bill 94
Florence, Wally 108

Flowers, Richmond 103
Foley, Tim 77
49ers, San Francisco 73, 74, 106, 119
Fresno State University 45

Georgia Tech 87-89, 97
Giants, New York 14, 36-40, 53, 55, 103, 106
Gouger, Morris 88
Grange, Harold (Red) 7, 17-22, 50, 65
Gray, Mel 103
Green, Cornell 81, 82
Green Bay Packers 14, 37, 41, 50, 53, 55, 68, 69, 80, 81, 106
Grim, Bob 35
Groom, Jerry 94
Groza, Lou (The Toe) 60

Halas, George 85, 86
Hall, Ken 7, 24-27
Harder, Pat 119
Harrisburg (Pennsylvania) Tech 98
Hart, Leon 94
Harvard 14, 33
Haskell Institute 28
Haven (Kansas) High 98
Hayes, Bob 103-106
Heisman, John 87
Henry, Wilbur (Fats) 66
Heston, Willie 10, 11
Hickey, Red 74
Hightower, L. V. 25

Hilltoppers, West Liberty 14-16
Hines, Jim 106
Hinkle, Clark 55
Hirsch, Elroy (Crazylegs) 41
Houston, Ken 78
Houston Lutheran 24
Houston Oilers 23, 27, 78
Hunter, Scott 80
Huston, Don 41, 110

Idaho, University of 73, 74
Illini 17, 19-22, 65, 79
Illinois, University of (Illini) 17, 19-22, 65, 79
Indians, Stanford 110
Interceptions 78-80
Irvin, LeRoy 119

Jets, New York 66-68, 106, 119
Johnson, Billy (White Shoes) 29, 30, 31
Johnson, Curley 66
Jones, Dub 119
Jones, Lam 106

Kansas 97
Kansas City Chiefs 35, 44, 46, 47
Kapp, Joe (Injun) 34, 35
Keene, Tom 60
Kenney, Bill 45, 46
Kerr, Andy 91
Khayat, Bob 74
Kinard, Bruiser 95

"King of the Hill" 103
Korshalla, Joe (Cueball) 14-16
Kramer, Kent 35

Lambeau, Curley 53
Langston (Oklahoma) University 28
Lee, Bruce 77
Lee, John 70-72
Lewis, Tommy 95
Lindsey, Dale 35
Lions, Detroit 45, 63, 73, 99-101, 103, 106, 119
Los Angeles Rams 41-43, 80, 106, 119
Luckman, Sid 34, 85
Lujack, Johnny 94

Manlove, Bill 30
Manuel, Lionel 39
Martin, Jim 94
Matheson, Bob 77
McAfee, George 86
McClinton, Curtis 45
McConkey, Phil 40
McCullouch, Earl 103
McGinn, Tommy 7
McLain, Mayes 28
McNeil, Charlie 119
McPhail, Buck 60
McQueen, Butch 87, 88
Mehringer, Pete 106
Miami 97
Miami Dolphins 77, 106
Michigan State 116, 118

Michigan, University of 9, 10, 13, 18, 19-22, 114-116
Minnesota Vikings 34, 35
Mitchell, Lydell 28
Moegle, Dicky 95
Montana State 64
Montgomery, Cleotha 28
Montgomery, Wilbert 28
Morehead State 38
Morris, Joe 39, 40
Mrs. Played Pro Football 108
Munn, Biggie 116
Mustangs 111

Nagurski, Bronko 52
Namath, Joe 68
Nance, Jim 58
Nebraska 95
Nesser brothers 112, 113
Nevers, Ernie 119
New England Patriots 58
Newman, Harry 53-55, 58
New Orleans Saints 59, 62, 63
New York Giants 14, 36-40, 53, 55, 103, 106
New York Jets 66-68, 106, 119
North Central College 48
North Park College 48, 49
Northwestern 19
Notre Dame 94, 114

Oakland Raiders 24, 103
Ohio State 106, 116
Oilers, Houston 23, 27, 78

Ole Miss 95
O'Neal, Steve 66-68
One-Game Wonders 119
Oosterbaan, Bennie 114-117
Orlando Panthers 108
Osborn, Dave 35
Osmanski, Bill 86
Owens, R. C. (Alley Oop)
73-75

Packers, Green Bay 14, 37,
41, 50, 53, 55, 68, 69, 80,
81, 106
Paige, Stephone 44-47
Palinkas, Pat 108, 109
Panhandles, Columbus 112
Panthers, Orlando 108
Parcells, Bill 39
Pass Records 32-48
Patriots, New England 58
Payton, Walter 119
Penn State 28
Peters, Frosty 64, 65
Philadelphia Eagles 28, 63,
76
Point-a-Minute Teams 9
Pool, Hampton 86
Prairie View A&M 78
Prep Teams 98
Punt Records 66, 70
Purdue University 108

Raiders, Oakland 24, 103
Rams, Cleveland 45
Rams, Los Angeles 41-43,
80, 106, 119

Rechichar, Bert 59, 60
Red Raiders, Colgate 91-93
Reds, Cincinnati 106
Redskins, Washington 74, 76,
84, 86
Reynolds, Bob 110, 111
Rice 95
Rice, Grantland 114
Rio Grande College 16
Rose Bowl 110
Rushing Records 50-58

Safeties 80
Saints, New Orleans 59, 62,
63
San Diego Chargers 44, 78,
119
San Francisco 49ers 73, 74,
106, 119
Sayers, Gayle 56, 119
Scarpitto, Bobby 68
Simms, Phil 36-40
Simpson, O. J. 53, 55-58
Sitko, Emil 94
Smith, Tommie 106
Snow, Neil 10
Southern Cal 92, 114
Southern Methodist
University 99, 110, 116,
117
Spartans 116
Stagg, Old Man 14
Stanford Indians 110
Stanford University 10, 110,
111
Stenerud, Jan 24

St. Lawrence University 91
St. Louis Cardinals 103, 118, 119
St. Mary's of California 97
Strong, Ken 53
Student Manager 32
Suffridge, Bob 76
Sugar Land (Texas) High School 24, 25, 27
Swanson, Bruce 48, 49
Sylvia High 98
Syracuse 95

Tampa Bay Buccaneers 55
Tennessee, University of 59, 76
Texas A&M 27, 66, 117
Thomas, Bob 119
Thompson, Bill 68
Thorpe, Jim 106, 107
Tinker, Gerald 106
Tittle, Y. A. 73
Todd, Dick 24, 25
Todd, Richard 119
Touchdown Records 9-32
Triplett, Wally 119
Tripucka, Frank 94
Turner, Bulldog 86

U.C.L.A. 70-72
Unitas, Johnny 23
Utah State 81
Utah, University of 61

Van Brocklin, Norm 41, 119

Vaught, Johnny 85
Versaci, Tony 117, 118
Vikings, Minnesota 34, 35

Wake Forest 52
Walker, Doak (The Doaker) 99-102
Warner, Glenn (Pop) 91
Washington, Gene 35
Washington Redskins 74, 76, 84, 86
Washington State Cougars 72
Waterfield, Bob 41, 119
West Liberty Hilltoppers 14-16
White, Whizzer 29, 31
Wilder, James 55
Williams, Bobby 94
Wolverines, Michigan 9, 10, 13, 21, 22, 114, 116
Woolfolk 55
Wyoming, University of 61

Yale 14, 32, 33
Yeager, Charley 32, 33
Yellowjackets, Cedarville 14, 15
Yost, Fielding H. (Hurry Up) 9, 20, 21
Young, George 38

Zaeske, Paul 48
Zuppke, Bob 20-22, 65

JAN 1 9 1988	DATE DUE	
OCT 5 1988	DE 12 '94	
NO 21 '88	AP 18 '95	
AP 17 '89	DC 3 '96 11/13	
OCT 27 '89	4.4 11/24	
FE 15 '90		
MY 25 '90		
JA 7 '91		
FE 25 '91		
DE 12 '91		